Dear Jan
I hope you enjoy this
Book
Lots of Love Aki
Sep 2007

Nader Angha:
Theory "I" - The Inner Dimension of Leadership
ISBN 1-904916-04-X

© 2002, 2006
by Maktab Tarighat Oveyssi Shahmaghsoudi (M.T.O.)®

Second revised edition 2006
First published in 2002

Editor:
MTO Shahmaghsoudi-Foundation,
Frankfurt a. M., Germany

British Library Cataloguing in Publication Data
A catalogue record for this book is available from the British Library.

Printed and bound in Great Britain by Antony Rowe Ltd.

For more information, please visit us at:
http://**www.mto.org**

Contents

Preface

What is "Leadership"? How can it be accurately defined? Is someone a born leader or can the quality of leadership be learned?

Science has examined the settings and levels of human organization and the definition of management in the stricter sense and leadership in the wider sense, from various different angles. The political sciences examine forms of government and develop theories on how best to structure, organize and administrate communities of human beings. The social sciences describe and examine the relationship between the individual and the community or society and consider possibilities of solutions to both internal and external difficulties and conflicts. The business management sciences combine the description of the organization and the optimal formulation of the factors of productivity with the description of human beings functioning within organizations, including the influencing factors.

Scholarship in these fields has yielded a voluminous body of literature, but compared to the rapid progress in "hard" sciences, such as chemistry, mathematics and physics, development in the human, behavioral sciences has been surprisingly slow. Only recently have scholars concluded that acknowledging the significance of the individual is essential to yielding optimal results in every setting, at every level. The recognition and development of individual human potentials is the single most important factor, and this perspective requires a different definition of leadership.

This book introduces the concept of Theory "I". In this theory, leadership is defined as "the creative capacity to evoke the most positive capabilities and potentialities within ourselves, and consequently, within others".

Theory "I" is based on the logical consideration that a wise person is one who gains benefits and avoids losses. Professor Angha explains that what is decisive here is what is used as the gauge for decision-making. He explains the necessity to base decisions on a gauge that is not subject to local, temporal or social changes. Theory "I" is about this gauge, which enables the leader to evoke the talents and potentials within him or herself and within others.

                                                    The Editors

1. An Overview of Management Theory

1.1. Science and the Scientific Method

Science (from the Latin *scire*, "to know") deals with knowledge. The development of scientific method can be described as a determined effort to systematize the process of acquiring knowledge so as to minimize the various pitfalls of observation and reasoning. Scientists use the scientific method to explain causal relationships among variables whose validity they take as factual. Talcott Parsons, one of the most eminent systems theorists of the twentieth century, claimed that the most important indication of development in any science is the existence of a systematic theory that explains concepts, major variables, and the rational composition of these variables.[1] The knowledge of scientific theory enables practitioners in every field to avoid past mistakes and to forecast, predict, and set reasonable goals before committing resources to achieve them.

A theory is a set of systematically interrelated concepts, definitions, and propositions that are advanced to explain and predict phenomena occurring in nature. Scientists theorize about observations they make. Their theories must consistently account for all observations and should have a logical structure. The rationalist approach has a significant role in scientific theory building. Scientists believe that all knowledge can be deduced from the laws of nature, and that these laws structure the world in a logical fashion.

To fully understand the implications of the scientific approach, we must first examine existing management theories and probe how the philosophy of management has changed over the years. Such a review will provide us with the background to develop a theory of management that is superior to existing approaches because it takes into account the potential of the individual.

1.2. The Evolution of Management Theory

In the past seventy years, the theory of management has undergone a number of far-reaching changes; the most important change is the recognition of the significance of human resources. Prior to this period, human resources were not identified as a major factor contributing to the success of an organization.

During the economic recession of the 1930s in the United States, workers' general dissatisfaction with their working conditions became evident in labor movements and strikes.[2] The Great Depression saw unemployment in excess of 25 percent. A limited market, overproduction, excessive competition, and poor merchandising methods crippled many industries. Manufacturers attempted to save money by reducing labor costs. The gradual accumulation of grievances against low wages, long working hours and new methods of production that entailed harder work, as well as the displacement of part of the work force from the industry brought about a collective rise of workers against their employers.[3]

As workers were being exploited, unrest and strikes ensued. Trade unions sought and gained major advantages for the working class. In the 1920s and 1930s, legislatures and courts actively supported organized labor, and workers attracted more attention. As a result, the emphasis was placed on understanding the workers and their needs - "it was the birth of the human relations movement."[4]

Organizations redirected their attention from non-human to human resources. In the 1930s, the critical stance of government and of numerous social groups toward private organizations forced managers to reconsider the nature of their work and to take into consideration the human aspects of management.

During World War II, the defense programs of the United States played an increasingly important role in the development of management theory. Factories were called upon to manufacture large volumes of products. The emphasis on efficient production gave a strategic importance to the function of management at any level of organization, and thus the progression of management took new forms. Management theories concentrated mainly on the internal market, but factors such as resource shortages coupled with advances in communication and transportation have recently led many companies to enter the international arena to expand their markets.[5] Therefore, industrial globalization has become one of the most important forces to influence management.[6] International competition, higher standards of quality, increased diversity, and the need to satisfy internal and external customers have had a major impact on leadership methods.

This section of text outlines the evolution of management. The different theories of management will be examined in chronological order, as indicated on the following time line.[7]

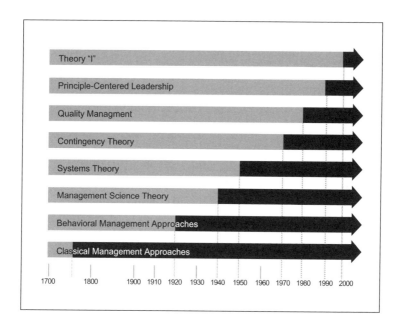

Figure 1: Time Line of Management Evolution

1.3. Classical Management Theory

The late eighteenth century Industrial Revolution initiated a shift from individual work to factory production. In its infancy, the new factory system posed many management challenges. New machinery in the factories necessitated the reorganization of managerial structures and manufacturing operations, as well as the retraining of employees. Moreover, managers had to deal with social dislocations caused by the transition from individual to industrial work. Managers had to develop solutions to meet these new challenges, which brought about the study of management theory in a field generally called Classical Management Theory. This field is comprised of three major sub-fields: the Classical

Scientific School, the Theory of Bureaucratic Organization, and the Classical Administrative School.[8]

1.3.1. The Classical Scientific School

Thinkers of the Classical Scientific School taught managers to apply scientific methods to solve factory problems. These methods emphasized a rational scientific approach to the study of management based on an orderly set of principles that replaced the old system of trial-and-error. The central thesis of this school was that an organized body of knowledge existed within organization management, and that it could be taught and learned. The goals were to make organizations efficient operating machines, and to make an efficient "organizational man" out of each employee. Man was considered to have a rational and economic nature.

The founder of Scientific Management Theory was Charles Babbage (1792-1871). In his essay, "On the Division of Labor" (1832), Babbage described his analytical approach to factory methods and costs, as well as his observations on the important principle of the division of labor.[9] He concluded that definite management principles existed, that these principles could be determined by experience, and that they could be applied broadly through the interchange of experience. He further emphasized that the division of labor among workers would increase labor efficiency and productivity because each individual would only have to master one particular task instead of multiple tasks.

Henry Metcalfe (1847-1917) introduced the concept of empiricism into management theory. He suggested recording the experience of a particular business so that its managers could study and learn from its successes and failures.

In 1885, he made the striking statement that "the administration of arsenals and other workshops are in great measure
an art, and depend upon the application to a great variety of
cases of certain principles, which taken together, make up
what may be called the 'Science of Administration'."[10]

Another pioneer of the Classical Scientific School was
Frederic Winslow Taylor (1856-1915). Taylor's theory
that labor productivity could be improved by scientifically
determined management practices earned him the status of
"Father of Scientific Management". Taylor applied scientific
management methods to factory problems. He believed
that with proper use of labor, tools, and time, it would be
possible to optimize management and productivity.[11] An
instructive example of Taylor's approach dates from the time
he worked for Bethlehem Steel of Pennsylvania in 1898. He
estimated that by streamlining movements and techniques,
workers could load about four times the amount of steel they
normally loaded. To get the workers to adopt his strategy,
he offered a higher rate of pay for meeting the higher quota.
In this way he succeeded in quickly increasing productivity.
He emphasized that labor efficiency and productivity could
dramatically increase by applying the findings of time-and-
motion studies, and that it was possible to achieve optimum
productivity by utilizing empirical data.[12]

Taylor further insisted that scientific management
was more than merely an efficiency device, or a motion-
study system. Increase in productivity required scientific
management, but without a concomitant change in the mind-
set of both management and workers, scientific management
could not work. Only when cooperation replaced strife and
antagonism could scientific management come to fruition.

Henry Gantt (1861-1919) shared many of Taylor's views. Gantt further advanced Taylor's views by advocating the importance of human elements in management. He insisted that knowing the methods and mastering the skills of management were essential, but that the willingness to apply and use the best method was at least as important. Gantt emphasized that teaching and leadership would be the management techniques of the future, compared to the prevailing method of driving workers to maximize production.[13] In other words, he advocated the concept of motivation, as it is known today. To motivate workers, he introduced the bonus system as a motivational tool.

Like Gantt, Frank Gilbreth (1868-1924) and his wife Lillian Gilbreth (1878-1972) were interested in the role of workers in the production process. Moreover, after analyzing work habits, they suggested reducing unnecessary movements and waste. In their famous studies on bricklaying, they reduced ten movements to five, thus doubling productivity. Their studies of hospital procedures reduced material waste and tightened time in operating rooms.[14] Frank Gilbreth believed that the standardization of every process, tool, and practice was a requirement for the success of scientific management. He emphasized that studies of motion, fatigue, skill, and time were essential for determining optimal ways to work.[15]

Lillian Gilbreth emphasized that under scientific management, "a task is determined through a complex process of analysis and synthesis. Analysis involves separation of constituent elements, and synthesis is the process of putting things back together and combining separate elements into a whole system."[16] She pointed out the importance for individuals to relate to organizational tasks in such a way that they contribute to the achievement of the grand purpose of the organization. This conceptual move from the individual task to the grand purpose had to be considered an "advanced and sophisticated recognition of a complex process, especially in the early days of Scientific Management."[17]

Assessment of the Classical Scientific Management School

The science of management benefited from several of the concepts developed by the early theorists of Classical Scientific Management. These theorists initiated a careful study of tasks and jobs to discover the optimal way to perform work; they demonstrated the importance of compensation for performance, and they emphasized the effectiveness of personnel selection and training. Today, managers still search for better ways to increase productivity without, however, agreeing on one universally valid solution.[18] In a situation where many changeable variables and factors influence the outcome, it seems impossible to find an optimal method.

Classical Scientific Management failed to realize the value of the human element in organizations. Lack of consideration for the human dimension was the single most important factor contributing to the failure of this method in the long term. Its goal was to increase the efficiency and the productivity of the workers by optimizing the work process. This school of management was one-dimensional in its way of thinking and it failed to realize the value of human nature, which it considered to be passive and mechanistic. There are many critics of the dehumanizing potential of scientific management. They agree that in this method, "the work of an employee was analyzed as one might analyze the operation of a machine, and the goal was maximization of efficiency of this 'human machine'".[19] With a typical Classical Scientific Management perspective, Taylor "looked at pig iron loaders, especially good ones, as strong, not particularly smart oxen. The controls and procedures he developed were testimonies to his mechanistic view of human nature".[20] Obviously, the "mental revolution" and the "concept of originality" that Taylor referred to were impossible to achieve within the limitations that his theory imposed on individuals' dignity and values.

Some of the pioneers of this school made positive contributions to management theory. Gantt's introduction of tasks and the bonus system replaced Taylor's piece-rate approach and was a move in the right direction, as was Gilbreth's departure from the specific task to the grand purpose of organization. Scientific Management improved productivity but failed to recognize the importance of social context and workers' needs. Therefore, it led to increased conflict between managers and employees, and workers often felt exploited.[21] Efficiency is as important today as it was a century ago. To survive in a world of global industrialization, efficiency must be the top priority of today's management. However, if managers do not realize the value of human beings, an organization's effectiveness and efficiency both become impossible.

1.3.2. The Theory of Bureaucratic Organization

This sub-field of the Classical Management school considers management as an impersonal and rational process that increases efficiency through devices such as record keeping, separating management and ownership, and clearly defining a hierarchy of authority and responsibility. The German sociologist Max Weber (1864-1920) introduced most of the concepts of Bureaucratic Organization. He theorized that large organizations in business, government, religion, and the military required a new type of management. His model of efficient organization was based on a hierarchical and rational process.[22] To Weber, rationality in an organization meant employee selection and advancement based on competence, rather than on nepotism, as well as on what he called "the use of rules, policies, hierarchy of authority, reward systems and other formal devices to influence employee behavior and assess performance."[23] Weber believed that an organization should not be managed in a traditional manner that stressed loyalty to leadership, but should rely on more rational bases. This school of management, with its rules and bureaucratic procedures, provided a standardized way of dealing with employees. "Rules, regulations, and procedures that [were] tried and shown to be valid [were] the bases for decision making and uniformly applied to all employees, ensuring a predictable result."[24]

Assessment of Bureaucratic Organization

Weber believed in management on an impersonal, rational basis. This method of management subjected individuals to rules and procedures that would ensure reliable, predictable behavior. Although management on a rational basis is an acceptable concept, the question remains: What is rational, and whose rationality are we referring to? Certainly, the reality of an individual's rationality is not being addressed in this theory.

To Weber, rationality had a limited meaning. He spoke of it as a means of differentiating one type of action from other types based on informational facts. To him, the rational manager was the manager who was informed.[25] This school of management considered individuals as passive, indifferent, and unwilling to take on responsibility; an organization needed to control workers by imposing rules and procedures. In such an organization, power must be used and integrated so well that it would encourage workers to give their voluntary support to the leadership. However, when rules and procedures are not in harmony with human nature and neglect the importance of the individual, adverse effects are unavoidable. It is therefore not surprising that the term bureaucracy has assumed a negative meaning in modern organizations, and is often associated with endless rules and red tape, low productivity, and the lack of a spirit of cooperation and collaboration.

1.3.3. The Classical Administrative School

Whereas the Classical Scientific School focused on the productivity of the individual worker, the Classical Administrative School studied the management of organizations. Yet, both schools share Taylor's premise that there are universal principles of management, and they can be taught and learned. While Taylor, a pioneer of the Classical Scientific School, studied the production process on the shop floor, the French mining engineer Henri Fayol (1841-1925) examined and applied these supposedly universal principles to top managers and administrators. In his most significant work, General and Industrial Management, Fayol discussed fourteen principles and five related functions of management that he considered to be general guidelines applicable to any organization.[26] Many of these principles had been known since the early days of the factory system, but Fayol was the first to integrate them into a comprehensive theory.[27] Since these principles are the base of current management theory, they will be cited in full:

Division of work: Specialization allows workers and managers to acquire an ability, sureness, and accuracy that will increase output. More and better work will be produced with the same effort.

Authority: The right to give orders and the power to exact obedience are the essence of authority. Its roots are in the person and the position. It cannot be conceived of apart from responsibility.

Discipline: Discipline comprises obedience, application, energy, behavior, and outward marks of respect between employers and employees. It is essential to any business. Without it, no enterprise can prosper.

Unity of command: An employee should receive orders from one superior only: one person, one boss. In no case can a social organization adapt to a duality of command.

Unity of direction: One head and one plan should lead a group of activities having the same objective.

Subordination of the individual to the general interest: The interest of one person or group in a business should not prevail over that of the organization.

Remuneration of personnel: The price of services rendered should be fair and satisfactory to both employees and employer. The level of pay depends on an employee's value to the organization and on factors independent of an employee's worth, such as cost of living, availability of personnel, and general business conditions.

Centralization: Everything that serves to reduce the importance of an individual subordinate's role is centralization. Everything that increases the subordinate's importance is decentralization. All situations call for a balance between these two positions.

Scalar chain: The chain formed by managers from the highest to the lowest is called a scalar chain, or chain of command. Managers are the links in the chain. They should communicate to and through the links as they occur in their chains. Links may be skipped only when superiors approve and a real need exists to do so.

Order: There should be a place for everyone, and everyone should be in his or her place; there should be a place for everything and everything in its place. The objective of order is to avoid loss and waste.

Equity: Kindliness and justice should be practiced by persons in authority to extract the best that their subordinates have to give.

Stability of tenure of personnel: Reducing the turnover of personnel will result in more efficiency and fewer expenses.

Initiative: People should be allowed the freedom to propose and execute ideas at all levels of an enterprise. A manager who is able to permit the exercise of initiative by subordinates is far superior to one who is unable to do so.

Esprit de corps: In unity there is strength. Managers have the duty to promote harmony and to discourage and avoid those things that disturb harmony.[28]

In addition to these fourteen principles of management, Fayol outlined five essential functions of management, according to which the manager's role would become one of planning, organizing, commanding, coordinating, and controlling the work of others toward organizational goals.[29]

Mary Parker Follett (1868-1933), who had a background in philosophy and social science, was another important contributor to the Administrative School of Management.[30] She studied organizational conflict resolution and managerial goal sharing, and emphasized the importance of worker participation. Follett was one of the first scholars to focus on an individual's importance within the organization. She developed the theory that workers operate best in teams, and that there is a scientific method of analyzing human relationships. Social context was a central issue in her theories. Furthermore, she emphasized that skills, principles, and professional managers were of paramount importance.[31] Follett stressed the group as the primary building block of the organization. She claimed that it was "only through relationships in groups with others that individuals could find their true identity and be totally creative."[32]

Follett further emphasized the importance of coordination and cooperation among the members of an organization. She outlined three strategies for settling differences between workers and management. With the first strategy, domination, one side wins and the other side losses. With the second strategy, compromise, neither side gets what it wants, and both sides remain unsatisfied. With the third strategy, integration, the dispute requires outside intervention whose goal is to find a new solution beyond the boundaries of the proposed alternatives.[33]

According to Follett, unifying a business required an understanding of integration as a way of settling differences, some system of cross-functioning to promote cooperation and coordination, and a sense of collective responsibility to give an organization coherence.[34] In her opinion, members of an organization would belong to the same group and therefore share common interests. "The attainment of the common interests of the organization's members [becomes] a ,"collective responsibility", and as the members work [...] together, the group attain[s] an 'integrative unity' or 'oneness'".[35] Follett believed that managers were responsible for developing the group's common purpose.

Chester Barnard's (1886-1961) contribution to the Administrative School of Management was his Acceptance Theory of Authority.[36] This theory emphasized that managers can only be effective if workers accept their superiors legitimate right to give commands. If, at the same time, those who receive commands do so willingly, they therefore exercise some kind of authority toward the managers. Thus, "the reality of authority", in Barnard's view, "has less to do with the managers and more to do with employees". Authority, according to Barnard, and contrary to popular belief, "flows from the bottom to the top of the organization".[37]

For Barnard, science could not be applied to every aspect of human interaction. He further maintained that organizations must learn to manipulate groupings and factions among their workers in order to improve the efficiency of the organization as a whole.[38] One of Barnard's major contributions was his conceptualization of an organization as a system by using concepts from the field of biology. By drawing an analogy to nature, he saw such a system as composed of many coordinated parts and activities of both internal and external environments. In spite of its compelling features, this concept did not gain recognition until the 1960s.[39]

Assessment of the Classical Administrative School

The first point that attracts one's attention to the Classical Administrative School's theories is their reconceptualization of the individual. While the Classical Scientific School presented the individual as an "organizational man", the Classical Administrative School presented the individual as a "social man." This school of thought put its emphasis on organizational environment and social context, therefore it postulated that the members of an organization had to cooperate and improve their relations in order to achieve the organization's goals. It would be possible to achieve personal objectives, but only so long as they contribute to the organization's goals. Recent developments in human relations theory have challenged the main principles of the Classical Administrative School. The principles of centralization, unity of direction, and scalar chain, for example, were replaced by a more participatory style of management.

In the Classical Administrative School of Management, Follett and other theorists defined the "social context of work and emphasized reliance on skilled, principled, and professional managers".[40] Follett's work was, in Merrill's words, "the point of convergence of the three broad channels of management philosophy. It include[d] the analytical, 'scientific' approach of Taylor, Gantt's emphasis on the importance of the human element, and Fayol's application of analysis to the field of administration."[41] Barnard moved a step further by conceptualizing organization as a social system and by elaborating on the origin of authority.[42] Classical Administrative Theory reflected the social conditions of its time. In general, it was assumed that man is by nature cooperative but inactive, and that in order to build effective organizations, emphasis has to be put on social relations and groups. On the other hand, the nature of organizations was considered to be active and independent of its members.[43] This school of management addressed issues such as ethics, power, and leadership strategies that would encourage employees to give their best.

While Classical Scientific Theory focused on production, Classical Administrative Theory was concerned with people and administration. However, the shortcomings of this management perspective were the centrality it gave to the social context of work, and what it considered to be the independent entity of the organization, which is separate from its members. This theory overlooked the fact that in reality every organization was composed of its members, and that the true nature of human beings was active, creative, and cooperative. In brief, this theory valued the social context of work, but ignored the individual worker and the capabilities of the human being, who is recognized only as a "social man". This is a limited view, but at least it points in the right direction.

1.4. Behavioral Management Theory

The Behavioral Management School considered workers as individuals with particular needs, as assets to be developed, and as important members of a larger societal group. Robert Owen (1771-1858), considered the "Father of Modern Personnel Management", wrote in 1813 that productivity was affected by the whole life of employees.

He believed that the conditions both on and off the job - the total environment - affected the volume and quality of a worker's output.[44] He was more than a century ahead of his time in discovering that it paid to devote attention to the welfare of humans as "vital machines", instead of treating them as "inanimate machines".[45] It was not until the 1920s that Mary Follett further elaborated on this concept. She directed attention to the human element within the social and administrative context of work, and emphasized the importance of people rather than engineering and administrative production techniques.[46]

Early works on industrial psychology and personnel selection received little attention because of the prominence of Scientific Management Theory. Behavioral Management Theory became popular after the Hawthorne Studies, led by George Elton Mayo (1880-1949) and conducted at a Chicago electric company in the 1920s. These experiments radically influenced management thought regarding human motivation. Mayo observed industrial workers on their jobs and came to the conclusion that "a sense of participation and feeling of being a member of a team are stronger motivating factors than economic self-interest, lighting, rest periods, and similar material influences".[47] Mayo believed that workers were individuals with unique wants, needs, goals, and motives, and therefore should be treated as individuals. He concluded that although the technical aspects of efficiency and productivity are important, the concern for process must be balanced with the concern for human beings and their needs.

While the methods and conclusions of the Hawthorne Studies have been questioned, they nevertheless had a profound impact on management theory because they altered the Classical Scientific School's rational and technical assumptions by stressing the human element in management. In other words, Mayo moved motivation theory away from the economic view of scientific management. He introduced innovative ideas regarding motives and individual differences, setting the stage for new research on human motivation.[48]

In general, theories dealing with motivation have one feature in common. They focus on how to stimulate individuals' interests and how to direct their energy toward higher performance. The major theories of motivation were divided into three major categories, Content Motivation theories, Process Motivation theories, and Reinforcement theory.[49] Content Motivation theories focused on the needs triggering motivated behavior. Based on this approach, managers could facilitate needed identification and satisfaction. Process Motivation theories, on the other hand, examined behavior, focusing on understanding how employees chose behavior to fulfill their needs. Reinforcement theory proposed that by understanding the consequences of behavior, good or bad, employees would be motivated to behave in desirable ways.

Abraham Maslow developed his Hierarchy of Needs theory in the 1940s. This theory was based on three assumptions: (a) human beings were wanting animals whose needs were never satisfied; (b) unsatisfied needs motivated human action; and (c) needs were arranged in a hierarchy best illustrated as a pyramid. As soon as needs at a lower level were satisfied, needs at a higher level would emerge.[50] Maslow's hierarchy of needs is presented in the following graph.[51]

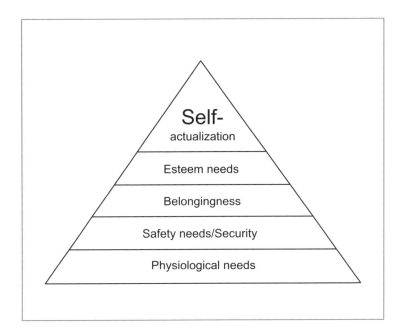

Figure 2: Maslow's Hierarchy of Needs

Maslow placed self-actualization at the top of the pyramid because the "self-actualizing individual sets goals and works to accomplish them, yet is guided by a set of principles and a code of ethics."[52] For its time, this was a revolutionary way of thinking about workers' needs because it made managers reevaluate the traditional belief that economic incentives were the primary motivation of all employees.

Victor Vroom introduced the Process Motivation Theory in the mid-1960s. His Expectancy Theory stated that an individual would evaluate various possibilities on the basis of anticipated work and reward before choosing or committing to a behavior. Therefore, a person's behavior would be influenced by the value of the rewards, the relationship of rewards to performance, and the efforts required by performance.[53] In other words, this theory defined human nature as rational; workers evaluated and calculated the wisdom of their behavior, based on their perceived value of the outcome.[54]

Also in the 1960s, Douglas McGregor synthesized the concepts of earlier thinkers in *The Human Side of Enterprise*.[55] McGregor's theory divided behavioral assumptions into two categories: Theory X and Theory Y. Theory X represented the traditional view of direction and control, portraying workers as essentially lazy and irresponsible, having to be forced to perform even the most basic tasks. Theory Y, which McGregor defined as a means of "integrating individual and organizational goals",[56] assumed that if workers operated in an adequate environment and knew the reasons for their work, they were inherently motivated and would work toward the fulfillment of their capabilities.

McGregor further emphasized that workers must be valued individually and recognize that they mattered to the organization. As a result, they would perform at a much higher level of responsibility and creativity.[57] McGregor suggested that an organization should de-emphasize formal authority and hierarchical structure, and place more emphasis on integration and creating conditions conducive to achieving personal and organizational goals.[58]

The School of Behavioral Management is still popular in managerial practice. Managers are very concerned with the needs and wants of their staff, and with helping their employees to develop their talents for the good of the organization. For the first time a school of management has integrated management with ideas from sociology, anthropology, and psychology.

Assessment of the Behavioral Management School

The major discovery of this school was that concern for workers' welfare and individuality led workers to commit to the organization, resulting in higher productivity. Applying behavioral sciences to management theory stressed that workers had many changeable needs and motives for their behavior. The Hawthorne Studies proved that productivity could be increased not only by physical factors such as improved lighting, but by psychological factors such as paying attention to workers' needs.[59] Realizing that individuals did not act in the rational manner that Weber had predicted,[60] managers often began to view their employees as individuals with various needs and expectations, and not "as nameless robots expected to follow orders blindly".[61] W. Jack Duncan summarized these changes in management theory as follows:

The image of human beings at work changes so dramatically from the writing of Taylor to the need theories of Maslow that one cannot help but wonder whether humans are really the object of both theories. The ox in Taylor's steel mill becomes the social creature at Hawthorne and perhaps even an angel or some similar almost divine being in Maslow's humanistic view.[62]

It is evident that a theorist's conclusions are determined by his view of human nature.[63] McGregor stated, for example, that managers' assumptions about the nature of individuals constituted the foundation of their management principles and leadership styles. As a result, the principle that derived from Theory X was that of direction and control through the exercise of authority.

Theory Y, in contrast, was based on the principle of integration.[64] However, this theory did not provide a guideline or a general formula for how such integration could be achieved. It implied that "organizations should take advantage of [the] imagination and intellect of all their employees",[65] but it is not clear how this could be implemented. Mayo also addressed this issue when he pointed out that one of an organization's primary goals is to "maintain 'spontaneous cooperation' throughout the entire structure".[66] In his view, the challenge was to develop ways for accomplishing these objectives.[67] Like McGregor, Mayo failed to provide a solid solution or guideline.

The Content and the Process Theories of Motivation and the Reinforcement theory all have limitations. For example, all regard action and reaction as the guiding forces of human behavior and provide satisfactory insights only on the surface. Content theories fail to take into consideration that all individuals are different, and that everyone has different needs and desires. Moreover, needs and motives constantly change. Process theories require managers to know each worker's expectations and desires and to respond to specific behaviors in order to produce motivation. Reinforcement theory focuses on changing and modifying the employees' on-the-job behavior through the appropriate use of immediate rewards and punishments. These theories focus on variables that are very diverse, changeable, and difficult to predict. The dominant view of management theory has been summarized as follows:

Successful managers recognize people as individuals and work with their particular differences. The successful manager knows that, because each of us is an individual, each of us is motivated differently. The more managers know about motivation, the more successful they will be in working with people.[68]

In other words, the task of managers is to develop innumerable motivational methods and plans in order to facilitate and satisfy the changeable needs and wants of a diverse group of employees.[69] This is almost impossible to achieve.

Increasingly, it became apparent that both groups oversimplified the problems facing management. The different theories and models of motivation failed to solve these problems and, due to their limitations, have only provided short-term remedies. Current theories of motivation address the changeable and limited aspects of individuals but ignore their inherent capabilities and therefore fail to provide satisfactory solutions for managers. Instead of emphasizing differences, one must discover common features in human individuals devoid of personal tastes and preferences, habits, geographical locations, ethnic and gender differences, and all other restrictions imposed by nature and the environment.

The limitations of McGregor's theory represent the shortcomings of the Behavioral School of Management, which claims that factors outside of the individual employees determine the success of an organization. A people-oriented theory of management does not necessarily mean that managers can motivate employees by creating a positive, supportive environment. Ultimately, motivation needs to be developed and cultivated within the individuals.

All individuals have the ability to empower themselves. Empowerment from outside is similar to pouring water into a well: it is merely a short-term remedy. Genuine empowerment happens when the water naturally erupts from the well. The Behavioral School took management theory one step further than the Scientific and Administrative Schools, but it, too, fell short of recognizing the reality of the individuals beyond their limitations, and failed to discover the most advantageous method of cultivating their goodness.

1.5. Management Science Theory

The advent of World War II provided the impetus for the next shift in management theory. Governments asked scientists in various fields to apply their knowledge to the problems of efficient large-scale weapons production and troop movement. The implications of such scientific approaches toward the war effort became evident after the war, when Henry Ford II reasoned that if mathematics and statistics could solve the problems of war, so could they solve the problems of management.[70]

As a result, the next wave of management theory shifted from concern for people as expressed by the Behavioral Management School to the use of quantitative methods. Turning their attention to helping managers make complex decisions, scholars developed the Normative Decision Theory.[71] This theory assumed that managers are satisfaction maximizers who knew all their options, as well as the outcomes associated with the various options, and could rank their preferences among the alternative choices they faced in a particular situation. In other words, they were "rational in the Weberian sense of being informed."[72] This kind of rationality required complete knowledge of all possible choices, outcomes, and consequences, as well as the collection and analysis of large amounts of data.

The invention of computers made a major contribution to the growth of management science. Used in conjunction with computers, management science now provides an objective supplement to the decision-making process, helping managers to clarify their logic and improve the quality of their decisions.[73] Some of the commonly used methods are forecasting, inventory modeling, linear programming, scheduling, and simulation analysis.

The aim of management science is to improve organizational effectiveness by reducing the risks involved in decision-making. The study of Management Information Systems (MIS) is the most recent sub-field of Management Science Theory. These systems are designed to provide relevant information to managers in a timely and cost-efficient manner.[74] The developments in MIS will be discussed in detail below in the section on Contemporary Management Theory.

Assessment of Management Science Theory

Between the end of World War II and the 1980s, managers were interested primarily in short-term results. Quantitative methods ensured that, in order to reap managerial bonuses for themselves, engineers and financial managers pushed their employees to their limits. In effect, post-World War II management theory disregarded the work of behavioral scientists. In the rush for quick profits, many American companies lost sight of the humanity of their workers. During that period a decision not based on a quantitative method was considered a poor decision. Companies became so preoccupied with scientific management models and techniques that they treated the organization as a closed system, operating in a vacuum independent of its environment. The emphasis on short-term results had two major negative implications. First, companies neglected long-term investment in research and development. Second, they focused on producing their products in the way they themselves wanted, overlooking changes in the market, ignoring customers' needs, and disregarding the importance of human creativity and insight.[75] Therefore, markets and whole industries were lost to foreign competition. The most dramatic effects of this policy could be witnessed in the American steel and automobile industries, which lost much of the domestic market to foreign competition.[76]

The Management Science approach provided tools for improved efficiency, but it could not replace managers' insight, creativity, and balanced decisions. The importance of management science should not be ignored, and it must be integrated into the decision-making process. However, management science is subject to a number of limitations. Most importantly, it cannot account for some aspects of decisions that are not quantifiable, such as creativity.[77] Another limitation of this approach was that it applied only to one phase of the decision-making process. It would be useless for identifying problems and developing alternatives.[78]

Management science is a useful tool for managers, but its overemphasis on quantitative methodology reduces its utility. Moreover, it mistakenly ignores or underestimates the human factor by over-relying on mathematical models and formulas.

1.6. Contemporary Management Theory

The most prevalent management theory at present is the behavioral management perspective. Contemporary theorists, however, have further developed this school into the following four sub-fields: Systems Theory, Contingency Management Theory, Quality Focus Theory, and Management Information Systems.

1.6.1. Systems Theory

In Systems Theory, an organization is an open organic system that interacts with its external environment and adapts to it. The theory teaches managers to take the whole organization into account when making decisions. According to Systems Theory, all components of an enterprise interact to create synergy, which can in turn benefit each component as well as the whole. Synergy is the benefit derived from the interaction of two or more elements. The synergy thus created exceeds the sum of the components individually.

Systems Theory requires an extensive informational structure to support its performance. Some of Systems Theory's concepts (such as synergy and open systems) have had a substantial impact on management theory, expanding managers' overall visions of their organizations. With the help of Systems Theory, managers noticed how the components of a system function:

- How the inputs of material, information, content, and energy derive from the external and internal environments;
- How the inputs are transformed into the outputs of products and services; and

- How the outputs are in turn discharged back to the environment.

It demonstrated how, through a feedback mechanism, these three phases function in a continuous and consistent way, how every system is constantly influenced by factors and forces in its internal and external environments, and how systems can be very complex.

Chester Barnard (1886-1961) was the first management theorist to examine organizations as systems, using concepts from the field of biology. In his view, a system was composed of the coordinated efforts and activities of many individual parts, each part was related to other parts, and the whole system differed in quantity and quality from the sum of its parts.[79] Barnard indicated that an organization could not be understood without reference to all factors in the external environment that interact with the organization and influence it. These factors included employees, suppliers, customers, and investors.

The power of Systems Theory, however, was not evident to most management theorists at first, and became popular only during the 1960s when the new realities of the market forced managers to apply its principles to every aspect of business.[80] Systems Theory led managers to think about quality as a concept affected by actions of various subsystems. Recent innovative methods that integrate different subsystems include:

- The "Just-in-Time" inventory-control system, which eliminates the need to store inventories by linking suppliers, manufacturers, and retailers.

– "Staying Close to Customers" approaches, which call for
   listening to customers inside and outside the company.

– The "Team Concept of Product Development", which
   integrates the activities of different management
   functions.[81]

In regard to feedback mechanisms, the emerging "360°
Feedback Model", also called multi-source assessment,
challenged the effectiveness of a single-source performance
assessment, assigning accountability not only to supervisors
but also to all stockholders, co-workers, and customers.[82]

A systems approach to management enhanced participatory decision-making of key forces such as employees,
suppliers, and customers. There were two main lessons for
managers to learn from Systems Theory. The first is that
no organization exists in a vacuum. The second lesson is
emphasizing the interrelatedness of different parts of an
organization, and their synergistic effect.[83]

Assessment of Systems Theory

The systems approach encourages managers to envision
their organizations as organic wholes. Changes in any
subsystems usually affect other subsystems and their
components. By keeping entire systems in mind, managers
hope to ensure that a positive move in one area does not
negatively affect another. The concept of an organization as
an open system implies the need to coordinate all subsystems
that constitute the organization. Linking a company's
suppliers to retailers, distribution centers, and corporate
headquarters is an example of a coordinated operation that
contributes to improved quality and decreased cost.[84]

All businesses are open systems and must interact with forces outside themselves. These environmental forces may require managers to modify their strategies. The interaction of an organization with its environment is a general rule of business that applies to all functional areas, such as operation management, marketing management, and strategic planning. In regard to marketing, the customer is always the central factor.[85] Focusing on the customer and customer satisfaction guarantees the success of the marketing plan. Although managers acknowledge that the customer is central to the success of a company, they have not yet recognized the critical value and role of the employee. It is important to remember that, as Graham states, an "organization is a social system composed of individuals."[86] The success and the survival of an organization can materialize only if the true value of the individual is recognized, and if managers make every effort to enhance workers' dignity and to improve their physical, mental, emotional, and spiritual well-being.

Like organizations, human beings, as organisms, are open systems. Changes in any one subsystem affect other subsystems as individuals constantly interact with their environment. A human being acquires input in the form of food, oxygen, mental activity, and energy, and is influenced by outside physical forces such as gravity. Inputs are processed by the whole system, which in turn generates outputs. In a state of equilibrium, an output is a balanced individual, who experiences physical, emotional, mental, and spiritual well-being. However, obstacles and limitations imposed on human beings and their inherent capabilities and potentials destroy the equilibrium of the whole organism. The concept of synergy also applies to individuals. Different aspects or elements of a human being interact and are interconnected to create synergy, which can benefit each element as well as the whole.

To sum up, for managers, employees should be at the core of the organization. The individual is the main source of energy, power, wisdom, dignity, and harmony. Systems Theory encourages managers to view their organization holistically. However, the basic rules of systems also apply to human beings, which are at the core of systems. Only when the reality of human beings is recognized can their interaction with their environment be determined.

1.6.2. Contingency Management Theory

The universalistic view of Classical Management theory assumes that there is an optimal way to handle any situation, and that every situation fits into a standard pattern. Business education, on the other hand, suggests that managers should evaluate each situation as it arises, since each situation is unique, and each case needs to be managed differently. There is some truth in each of these approaches, but neither one is entirely correct. The Contingency Model seeks to remedy the shortcomings of both theories.[87] According to this model, certain contingencies exist in different situations, and managers are responsible for identifying key contingencies and developing plans suitable to deal with them. The main strength of Contingency Management is that it recognizes the complexity of management.[88] Rather than relying on universal principles of management, this approach focuses on the situational factors that affect the managerial process. "The crucial point is to determine the circumstances under which certain managerial actions will yield a particular set of results."[89]

Contingency concepts derive their strongest empirical support from fields such as leadership and organization design. In organization design, the roots of the situational theory of management go back to the 1930s. In 1931, Henry Sturgis Dennison, himself influenced by Classical Organizational Theory, insisted that the principles of organization were good only insofar as they would make the operation more productive. Dennison recognized the need for different degrees of centralization. Further elaborating on the situational theme, he introduced the concept of "continuous reorganization".[90] Continuous reorganization implies that an organization must restructure itself continuously in order to meet the realities of a changing environment.

The implications of Contingency Theory for Management become obvious in the approaches by Fiedler and by Paul Hersey and Kenneth H. Blanchard, who link leadership styles with specific organizational situations as well as with the readiness of employees to perform assigned tasks.[91] Fiedler analyzed the environment in which leaders function, and the way they exercise leadership.[92] He suggested that a manager choose a method of leadership that either emphasized tasks or focused on employees, depending on three situational variables:

- Leader-member relations - that is, the degree to which a leader is accepted by the group;

- The task structure - that is, the nature of the task, based on its simplicity, variety, complexity, or latitude for creative expression; and

- The power of the leader - that is, his or her ability to exercise influence inside the organization.

Hersey and Blanchard's approach to determining appropriate leadership behavior focused on the characteristics of employees and their readiness to perform tasks. They argued that employees vary in their readiness, based on their skills, confidence, and abilities. Therefore, leadership style should be contingent on the situation. The four leadership styles of telling, selling, participating, and delegating depend on the readiness of the employees.[93]

The Contingency Theory's importance is evident in a global environment and in the context of international competition. More recent Contingency Theories synthesize various elements from other theories of management. An example of such a synthesis is "Theory Z" by William G. Ouchi, who merged the traditional American and Japanese ways of managing people.[94] This theory recommends that American managers apply elements of Japanese management, such as consensual decision-making and a holistic concern for employees and their families.[95]

Assessment of Contingency Management Theory

The Contingency Theory of Organization emphasizes that an organization and its management methods should conform to situational factors. In this theory, an organization is treated as an open system, which is in constant interaction with its environment. Therefore, Contingency Management Theory emphasizes that the best way to manage is determined by contingencies present at a particular time or in a particular situation.

Obviously, management has moved from the absolute to the relative. Contingency Theories were a radical departure from Classical Management Theory. Originally, the "holy grail of Taylor, Gilbreth, and even Mayo was the mystical best way of doing management activities".[96] In contrast, Contingency Theory emphasized that there is no optimal way to manage. The critical point was identifying the key factors and variables in each situation. Only by determining these specific variables or contingencies can a manager apply certain managerial actions to obtain the desired results.[97] For tangible situational factors, such as new technology or operation management techniques, the application of contingency methods of management is possible and very effective. However, the intangible situational factors, the human aspect of an organization, are very complex. Particularly in a situation of industrial globalization, the application of contingency management principles is a very challenging task.

Because of Japan's industries worldwide economic success until the early 1990s, the Japanese system of management has been widely studied and copied in recent years.[98] However, due to many cultural differences between the United States and Japan, a complete imitation of the Japanese style of management is impossible. As discussed above, Ouchi's "Theory Z" of management integrates principles of American and Japanese management styles. Since cultural differences pose insurmountable obstacles to the integration of American and Japanese styles of management, the dichotomy between the individualistic and the collectivistic approaches to responsibility has remained intact. It is necessary to rely on the most efficient equipment and technology to remain competitive. But in regard to intangible cultural elements such as values, norms, and social interactions, the integration of two different methods of management is difficult to accomplish.

Current Contingency Theories suggest that leadership style must correspond to each situation. For example, Hersey and Blanchard recommended resorting to styles of "telling" and "selling" when the level of employees' maturity or readiness to perform tasks are low.[99] However, recent management theory encourages participatory management on all levels and in all situations, emphasizing employee empowerment, continuous improvement, teamwork, and so on.

Contingency Theory realizes that management is a complex task, but the proponents of this approach disagree over what is the most efficient management style. Without finding a consensus, it will be impossible to achieve integration, harmony, and cooperation, and management theories will have little implications for real life. We need to address a dimension of human existence that transcends all differences and contrasts. It is necessary to discover and develop a human dimension beyond layers of cultural, gender, and social differences - a dimension that is stable and reliable. The realization, discovery, and development of such a dimension will enable us to provide a formula that applies to any individual in any setting. Reacting to changeable variables and environments is not as productive as getting access to the constant and unchangeable dimension of human beings. The discovery, cultivation, and development of this dimension should be the goal of scholarly inquiry.

1.6.3. Total Quality Management (TQM)

America's incredible economic growth during the 1960s and 1970s created massive organizational and production structures. Many industries were more interested in producing large quantities of goods than in improving the quality of goods and services. Consequently, American manufacturers were unable to export their products in sufficient quantities. On the other hand, Southeast Asian countries, most notably Japan, sold massive amounts of their products on the U.S. market. This soon led to a huge trade imbalance. To remain competitive, American industries tried to improve the quality of their goods. The theoretical foundation of this reorientation was Total Quality Management (TQM).

TQM is a philosophy of organization-wide commitment to continuous improvement, with a focus on promoting teamwork, increasing customer satisfaction, and lowering costs. It encompasses horizontal collaboration across functions and departments within an organization, and includes customers and suppliers as well. This approach recommends that teams of workers be trained and empowered to make decisions that help the organization achieve high standards of quality. This constitutes a revolutionary innovation in regard to company-wide worker participation in corporate culture. In order to implement these changes, the mind-set of both managers and employees must change. TQM implies a shift from a centralized to a decentralized method of management.

The quality revolution spread throughout the 1980s and 1990s as executives saw quality improvements as the route to restoring global competitiveness. Interestingly, the founder of TQM, W. Edwards Deming, tried to introduce the concept in the United States in the early 1940s, but industry leaders ignored it. Instead, the Japanese adopted it after he presented it to corporate leaders in that country.[100]

Total Quality Management involves the use of many techniques. Some of its major elements include: employee involvement, focus on the customer, bench-marking, continuous improvement, and empowerment.[101] This approach asserts that the traditional style of management limits employee capabilities. Successful companies empower their employees, giving them what Daft calls "the power, freedom, knowledge, and skills to make decisions and perform effectively".[102] The concept of *Kaizen*, a Japanese management technique, focuses on developing systems for continuous improvement through employee suggestions. However, it emphasizes that high-quality ideas can be assured only if the organization is able to move the employees' hearts that is, give them the willingness and motivation to pursue continuous improvement.[103]

Assessment of Total Quality Management

Although TQM comes yet another step closer to what might be an ideal management methodology, it too is not the perfect solution. A recent survey of corporate leaders showed that two-thirds of the executives polled are dissatisfied with the overall results of utilizing TQM.[104] The most limiting factor for the implementation of TQM is the lack of commitment of the people in the organization. It only works when people want it to work. In other words, the human factor is the most critical element in the success of this method of management. The early development of TQM centered on three basic concepts: tools, training, and techniques. Over time, managers learned that focusing on only three concepts had a limited impact on quality. A critical element was missing.

For TQM to work, it must become an integral part of organizational culture.[105] This can only happen when the vast majority of workers in an organization demonstrate a daily commitment to the principles of TQM. Whether quality is reflected in a product or in a service rendered to the customer, it is the result of an action by one or more employees. Quality is therefore the result of positive employee behavior.

TQM integrates different theories of management. On one hand, improving the production process while decreasing cost builds on Management Science Theories. On the other hand, some elements originate in Classic Administrative Theories, such as the emphasis on the social aspects of work. Again, the focus is on the process and on the social dimensions of the work. TQM stresses the empowerment of the employees through common goals and strong corporate culture.

In an increasingly global environment with a diverse workforce, common goals have different meanings for different groups of employees. Workforce diversity is inevitable, and in a diverse environment, promoting diversity, empowering employees, and creating a unified corporate culture are challenging tasks for managers to accomplish. In such an environment, managers are ultimately the facilitators of personal and organizational development and transformation.

The fundamental questions remain unanswered: What is the force that empowers individuals and unleashes their energy, commitment, and enthusiasm? What provides the individual and eventually the whole organization with a sense of mission and coherent philosophy that unites and binds them together for the achievement of a common goal? Is there a higher dimension of the inherent capabilities of individuals, beyond artificial boundaries and limitations imposed by culture, society, race, gender, and ethnicity, which can be discovered and provide us with a formula to empower and manage ourselves and others?

1.6.4. Management Information Systems (MIS)

An information system is a set of people, procedures, and resources that collect, transform, and disseminate information in an organization.[106] Until the 1960s, the role of Information Systems (IS) within an organization was relatively simple; IS dealt mainly with transaction processing, accounting, record keeping, and other Electronic Data Processing (EDP) applications. Then another role came into play, the concept of Management Information Systems (MIS). MIS was conceived to focus on supporting the information requirements of managers in their decision-making process by providing predefined management reports.

By the 1970s, it was obvious that the pre-specified information products were not adequately meeting many of management's decision-making needs, so the idea of Decision Support Systems (DSS) was conceived. DSS provided interactive ad hoc support tools for decision-making processes; managers could produce reports based on criteria they specified in addition to the standard, pre-defined reports that were available. In the 1980s, Information Systems took on a new role. Microcomputers, application software packages, and telecommunication networks brought about the marvel of end-user computing. Managers could keep their own databases, create and modify their own spreadsheets, and etceteras.

To further help top corporate executives, the concept of Executive Information Systems (EIS) came about.

EIS enabled top executives to obtain the critical information they wanted, at any time they needed it, and in any format they preferred. Another breakthrough was made in the area of Artificial Intelligence (AI) and its business applications. As a result, Expert Systems (ES) and other knowledge-based systems emerged.

Strategic Information Systems (SIS) blossomed in the 1980s and continued into the 1990s. IS was no longer just an information utility; it became a producer of information-based products and services that earned profits for organizations and also gave those using SIS a competitive advantage in the marketplace.[107] Cybernetic systems, which have feedback and control components (self-monitoring and self-regulating), and other similar concepts, systems, and tools were developed to support the needs of MIS.

Since late 90's, the information system and its management have taken a more global role. The demand for global communication tools, their convenience and mobility has encouraged a tense competition amongst the high technologycompaniestocomeupwithfastertomarketproduct plans and therefore products that enhance the E-commerce business which has shown to be the trend of the new millennium.

"With the ability for a mass of people to achieve instant communication, also comes the increased consumer need for instant gratification from these same devices. People want their information, and they want it now. Satisfying the need, whether for information, for data, or for m-commerce (mobile electronic commerce), unleashes unlimited possibilities for the entrepreneurial business person."[108]

Managing vast amounts of data and information throughout a global supply network requires an entirely different set of skills than does implementing a software solution.[109] These sets of required skills asks for a new type of worker who can be more flexible to adjust to new environments and situations by presenting the capacity to learn and self-manage on a continuous basis.

1.6.5. MIS and the Human Factor in the New Millennium

MIS introduced knowledge workers, a new classification of workers who are defined as people who spend most of their workday creating, using, and distributing information.[110] They include executives, managers, engineers, secretaries, teachers, and many others. In short, all individuals within an organization are knowledge workers aided profusely by advances in technology.

Technology vendors are selling new technologies, such as data mining, intranets, video conferencing, and web casting, as "cure-all" solutions for the business challenges of the knowledge era. Trade press coverage of this modern "productivity paradox" has pushed the IT bandwagon on by suggesting that increasing investments in new information technologies would guarantee improved business performance. Some technology experts and academic scholars, however, are quick to point out that investments in IT do not guarantee greater business performance or knowledge management. Erik Brynjolfsson, a professor of information systems at MIT's Sloan School, for instance, noted that: "The same dollar spent on the same system may give a competitive advantage to one company but only expensive paperweights to another."[111] Hence, in order to receive higher return on an IT investment it is critical that information as it relates to organizational performance is used effectively.

The way in which industry executives achieve effective utilization of this information, however, remains an elusive issue, subject to as many opinions as there are "gurus" and vendors who sell them. Xerox Palo Alto Research Center Director John Seely Brown points out that in the last 20 years, U.S. industry has invested more than one trillion dollars in technology but has realized little improvement in the efficiency or effectiveness of its knowledge workers.[112] The gap between IT expenditures and organizations' business performance may be attributed to a transition from an era of competitive advantage based on information to one based on knowledge creation. The earlier era was characterized by relatively slow and predictable change that could be deciphered by most formal information systems. During this period, information systems based on programmable recipes for success were able to deliver their promises of efficiency based on optimization for given business contexts.

Brian Arthur, Dean of Economics and Population Studies at Stanford University, argues that the new world of knowledge-based industries is distinguished by its emphasis on precognition and adaptation, in contrast to the traditional emphasis on optimization based on prediction. Arthur suggests that the new world of knowledge-based business is characterized by "re-everything", re-organizing and re-engineering, for example. It would involve a continuous redefinition of organizational goals, purposes, and an organization's way of doing things. This new business environment would be characterized by radical and discontinuous change and it would demand anticipatory responses from organization members who need to carry out the mandate of a faster cycle of knowledge creation and action based on this new knowledge.[113]

In an information age characterized by relatively predictable change, technology gurus and hardware and software providers offer out-of-the-box solutions that are sold as a way to enable knowledge management. Such solutions are expected to offer the means for storing pre-defined recipes in information databases, which may be later used for crunching out the pre-determined solutions, based on pre-defined parameters.

Today's business world puts a premium on understanding and adapting to the changes in the game as well as the game itself; and knowledge management caters to the critical issues of organizational adaptation, survival, and competence in face of an increasingly dynamic environment. Organizational processes that seek synergistic combination of data and the information-processing capacity of information technologies, and, most of all, the creative and innovative capacity of human beings are the critical success factors.

Traditionally, information systems worked by seeking a consensual interpretation of information based on the mandate of company bosses. Such a mandate usually reflects a rigid, "we've always done it this way" attitude that ultimately confuses the concepts of knowledge and information. Knowledge and information, however, are distinct entities. Information generated by computer systems is not a very rich carrier of human interpretation for potential action; knowledge resides in the user's subjective context.

Noted expert Karl Erik Sveiby asserts that business managers need to realize that unlike information, knowledge is embedded in people, and knowledge creation occurs in the process of social interaction.[114] Likewise, Ikujiro Nonaka, the first Xerox Distinguished Professor of Knowledge at University of California, Berkeley, emphasizes that only human beings can take the central role in knowledge creation. Nonaka argues that computers are merely tools, however great their information- processing capabilities may be.

The new world of business imposes the need for variety and complexity of interpretations of information outputs generated by computer systems. Such variety is necessary for deciphering the multiple world views of the uncertain and unpredictable future. Strategy guru Gary Hamel underscores the significance that nonlinear change imposes upon organizations and the need for devising non-linear strategies. Such strategies cannot be predicted based on a static picture of information residing in the company's databases. Rather, such strategies will depend upon developing interpretive flexibility by understanding multiple views of the future.[115] In Hamel's perspective, the objective of business strategy would not be to indulge in long-term planning of the future. Rather, the emphasis would be placed on understanding the various future world views using techniques, such as scenario planning and action based on that information. Hence, it would be correct to suggest that knowledge resides in the user and not in the collection of information. The user's creativity and intuition is the determining success factor.

To meet the challenges of MIS in the new millennium, management needs to distinguish between explicit and tacit knowledge. Explicit knowledge is the objective and material knowledge that can be drawn from hard data. In other words, it is in black and white. Tacit knowledge, on the other hand, is subjective and experienced-based knowledge and is rooted in beliefs, images, and intuitions. It is the "gray area." Managers need to give more explicit recognition to tacit knowledge and related human potentials to develop a richer conceptualization of knowledge management.

Managers need to develop a greater appreciation for their intangible human assets captive in the minds and souls of their knowledge workers. Discovering and unleashing the hidden potentials of the knowledge workers' talents and creative abilities such as:

- *Acuity:* The ability to see the business environment more clearly and respond to the evolving needs and wants of various customers.

- *Agility:* The ability to adapt simultaneously to many different business environments.

- *Speed:* The ability to respond quickly to customer demands.

- *Consistency:* The ability to maintain focus and foresight in the midst of chaos.

- *Creativity:* The ability to create new values and generate new ideas.

Without these assets, companies are simply not equipped with the vision to foresee or to imagine the future.

Elevating computerization to the level of a magic bullet may diminish what matters the most in any enterprise: educated, committed, creative, and imaginative individuals working for organizations that place a greater emphasis on people'screativecapacitythanontechnologies.[116] Knowledge workers are under tremendous physical, mental, and emotional stress. They are so preoccupied and overwhelmed with daily pressures and uncertainties of the various factors in the environment, that tapping into their creative potentials and being proactive becomes an unachievable goal. Besides the above challenges, "the knowledge worker faces many health issues, such as job stress, damaged arm and neck muscles, eye strain, radiation exposure, cumulative trauma disorder, repetitive strain disorder, and even death, due to computer-related stress".[117] New ways of tapping knowledge workers' talents and creative abilities need to be implemented.

O'Brien notes that the use of IT in business has major impacts on society, raising serious ethical considerations in areas such as privacy, crime, health, working conditions, and individuality.[118] He explains that people may evolve in their motivational alignment through several levels of ethical reasoning, as indicated in the following illustration:

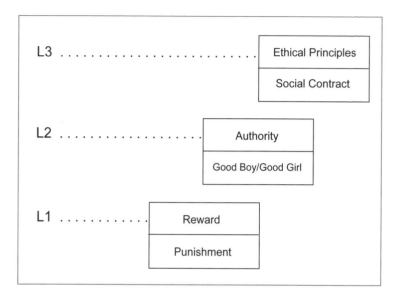

Figure 3: O'Brien's Stages of Ethical Reasoning and Motivation

In this model, it is assumed that when a person reaches the final stage of moral evolution, his or her actions are guided by self-chosen ethical principles (which usually value justice, dignity, and equality), not by fear, guilt, social pressure, and so forth. Therefore, such a person is productive, healthy, and motivated. However, reaching the final stage of moral evolution does not guarantee the expected outcomes. Many people with strong ethical principles who value justice, dignity, and honesty are still not motivated or empowered.

The mere recognition of these principles does not lead to their implementation.

In this new world of business characterized by high levels of uncertainty and inability to predict the future, the focus is not on finding the right answers but on finding the right questions. Being proactive and motivated is the key to success. Knowledge workers live in a dynamic environment that changes constantly; therefore, their survival is based on their ability and willingness to accept increased responsibility and on their willingness to be proactive. However, to access and cultivate the creative capacity and inner potentials, an individual needs to be in a state of balance, harmony and well-being.

Assessment of Management Information Systems

The behavioral part of MIS focuses on harmonizing IT to support individual and organizational goals. However, the burden of such harmonization falls on the individual employee. O'Brien states that despite faster cycle times, lean production techniques, new communications and data processing systems, it still comes down to the individual worker.

If the worker has not accepted the new company philosophy, has not consented to lifelong training, perpetual change and greater personal responsibility, then no new equipment or management pronouncements will make any difference. Harmonization cannot be forced nor induced. It must be voluntary.[119] The burden is on the individual employee to cope with the pressures and at the same time to be energetic, to be motivated, and to be proactive.

It seems that "the old motivational tools have lost their magic. The great challenge that lies before us is to restructure how we do work and reward people".[120] Even though, from a management point of view, MIS may improve sales and profits, decrease process costs, enhance operational efficiency, and provide short term competitive positioning advantage, the human factor is lost in the equation more than ever. Davidow and Malone call knowledge workers "lost souls".[121]

Current motivational tools focus on the social aspects of work; the focus is on the individual as "social man". The predominant assumption is that the disconnection between IT expenditures and the firm's organizational performance is due to the organization's ignorance of ways in which knowledge workers communicate and operate through the social processes of the organization. The focus needs to be shifted from the social aspects of the work environment to the individual person, and most of all, the creative and innovative capacities of human beings are the critical sucan factors; but attempts so far have been superficial and inadequate, for they do not address the individual's inner Self.

The new Information Technology system and its management will take its toll on workers if the problem is not addressed soon. The technology is moving too fast for the average person to keep up with the changes. If managers do not understand the true nature of their workers, balance in the workplace will be lost. Technology-related health issues and increased work demands for knowledge workers, as well as the loss of agility and creativity will continue to affect people's personal lives and society as a whole if workplace changes are not made.

1.7. Organizational development and transformation

This historical review of management theories has demonstrated that they evolved over time, and they aimed at enabling organizations to meet the challenges of an increasingly competitive marketplace. Improvements in an organization's performance are the result of carefully planned changes. Such changes occur at the macro and the micro level of an organization. Changes on the macro level focus on the organization as a whole. Issues such as organizational vision, mission, guiding principles, goals and strategies fall into this category. Changes on the micro level focus on the role of the individual. Social factors, such as corporate culture, teamwork, organizational structure and employees' needs satisfaction belong to this category.

Most managers believe that the macro and micro level complement each other and that organizational effectiveness and efficiency can only be achieved when both levels are considered simultaneously. However, a closer look at the limited way in which both macro and micro levels operate reveals that regardless of their names they both rely on a macro approach.

Both emphasize organizational behavior, and social interactions. Both focus on the organization's environment, and try to assess how the individual reacts to social and environmental factors, and both follow an outside-in approach. Even when the micro perspective deals with issues on an individual level, such as employees' needs satisfaction, it still deals with the organization's needs and the dominant social factors. The employees do not initiate the action; they only react to what has been determined by the organization. All actions are defined by the role the organization assigns. Employees only meet those expectations that their role requires them to fulfill. Since the focus is on the assigned role and not the individuals holding the role, their behavior is not a genuine response. It does not originate from their inherent capabilities and potentials. Consequently, they are neither empowered nor creative.

The discipline that guides the macro perspective is sociology. Therefore, the focus is on the social structure, role expectations, cooperation, and interaction among individuals. The micro perspective, on the other hand, is rooted in psychology. This perspective focuses on the individual as a member of an organization. It deals primarily with individuals' perceptions of an organization's vision and principles and studies how the individual reacts to the stimuli provided by an organization for the purpose of needs satisfaction and empowerment.

The macro and the micro perspectives are the basis of current major motivational theories. Process theories of motivation take a macro perspective and analyze the job process, employee expectations, and behavior modification. Content theories of motivation are based on a micro perspective. They study individuals and their needs satisfaction. However, both groups of theories are limited to situational factors and individual needs that change constantly. Consequently, they provide only temporary solutions.

A Planned Change Model developed by Jerry I. Porras and Robert C. Silver elucidated the mechanisms of planned change.[122] Most such models focus either on macro or micro perspectives. However, this Planned Change Model provides a significant advancement in combining the micro and macro perspectives. The following section of this chapter will briefly summarize its main themes and critically assess its implications for the individual worker.

1.7.1. The Planned Change Model

The Planned Change Model distinguishes two strategies of managerial intervention to improve efficiency and effectiveness. On the micro level, the strategy of Organizational Development (OD) aims to improve the work setting, for example, the structure of the organization, its physical setting, the technology used, as well as social factors such as corporate culture, worker interactions, teams, and management style.

On the macro level, the strategy of Organizational Transformation (OT) addresses the possibility for change in the organization's vision, such as its guiding beliefs and principles, its general purpose, and its mission. Successful Organizational Transformation results in a fundamental reorientation of an institution's behavior in the marketplace, and the adoption of innovative methods. While both strategies have to be applied simultaneously, the impacts of OT on overall changes in the organization outweigh those of OD.

The implementation of both OT and OD entails cognitive changes for the individuals concerned. However, OT reaches a deeper level and creates a paradigm change. Different individuals are affected differently by these changes. In turn, the cumulative effect of changes in behavior will vary. A successful implementation of OD and OT results in improved organizational behavior and enhanced individual development, both of which influence and reinforce each other. The diagram on the next page elucidates the principles of the Planned Change Model.

Assessment of the Planned Change Model

This model identifies the key components of organizational change and distinguishes between the major areas of an organization targeted by the OD and OT intervention strategies. The strategy of Organizational Development focuses on work setting variables and tries to implement changes by modifying environmental and social factors.

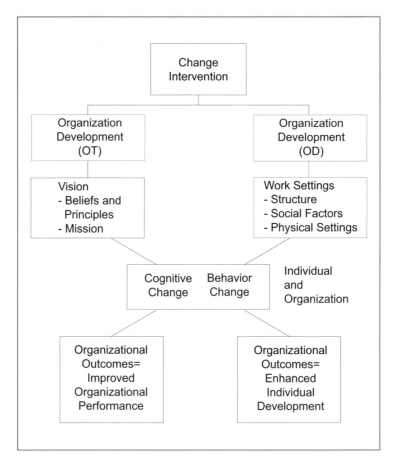

Figure 4: Planned Change Model

The individual as an agent of change does not factor in this strategy. Changes in the variables targeted by Organizational Transformation approaches (beliefs, purpose, and mission of the organization) are supposed to reach a deeper level.

However, this model fails to clarify the major differences between the micro and macro approaches because both OT and OD strategies follow an outside-in approach. Both strategies focus on factors in the environment and assess how they influence the perception, the belief, and the behavior of the individual. They do not consider the individual as an agent of permanent, self-perpetuating, and unprecedented changes. In reality, change occurs when enough members of an organization change their consciousness. Personal transformation leads to organizational transformation.

In regard to changes in individual consciousness, A. Levy and V. Merry (1986) identify two distinct approaches, of "Reframing" and "Consciousness Raising". Reframing results from managerial interventions that change a member's perception of reality. Reframing does not change current organizational reality; instead, it alters the way individuals view the world. This new world view leads to corresponding changes in attitudes and behaviors. Consciousness raising makes the process of transformation visible to the members of an organization. Techniques such as meditation and creativity exercises facilitate this strategy.[123] Levy and Merry suggest further exploring ideas from Asian philosophy and using Eastern concepts of the individual for theories of Organizational Transformation.[124]

In summary, Planned Change Models fail to provide a model for successful cognitive change because they neglect the role of the individual. Organizational Transformation requires individual transformation; it requires that one moves beyond the borders of one's current level of consciousness and discovers higher levels of consciousness.

1.8. Principle-Centered Leadership

Recent theories in the field of management include Principle-Centered Leadership, Exemplary Leadership and others. Stephen Covey developed Principle-Centered Leadership around 1990 and it enjoys widespread popularity among corporate leaders. Surprisingly, this theory received little scholarly attention and academic textbooks make almost no reference to it. The Principle-Centered Leadership theory redirects its attention from the work process and its social context to the workers themselves, making leadership and vision at the individual level its principle concern. It therefore recognizes the role of the individual as the cause of change in the organization. No longer are workers' preassigned roles or the social context of the organization the catalysts for change.

Another leadership model, "Exemplary Leadership" introduced by Kouzes and Posner, identifies five fundamental practices that enable leaders to achieve success. The practices include: challenge the process, inspire a shared vision, enable others to act, model the way, and encourage the heart.[125] This model expresses that excellence rises from within; it cannot be imposed from without. Leadership is defined as the art of mobilizing others to want to do the job. Encouraging the heart in this leadership framework implies that the secret of success is love. Leaders cannot achieve extraordinary things without having their hearts in it. The word "encouragement," after all, has its root in the Latin word *cor*, meaning heart.

These and other similar models attract attention to the individual and provide a paradigm change in management theory. Covey's principle-centered leadership introduces a radically new model that challenges the current consensus among management theorists. Such a paradigm shift is of utmost importance because it emphasizes that change and development originates from the individual and then penetrates to the environment. Covey introduces the concept of "character ethic", with its constituent elements of fairness, integrity, service, justice, and simplicity:

"The character ethic is based on the fundamental idea that there are principles that govern human effectiveness natural laws in the human dimension that are just as real, just as unchanging and unarguably 'there' as laws such as gravity are in the physical dimension."[126]

He believes that these principles resemble natural laws and therefore cannot be changed, and the recognition of the principles of character ethic will inevitably lead to a paradigm shift in management theory.

Covey notes that since World War I, there has been a shift in the general view of success from character ethic to personality ethic. Personality ethic values quick and easy ways to achieve quality of life and personal success. It's main methods were human and public relation techniques, power strategies, and the creation of a positive mental attitude. Principle-Centered Leadership challenges such traditional approaches and makes the individual its point of departure. Considering the current state of management theory, this challenge is tantamount to a paradigm shift.

Paradigms, Covey explains, are a set of unalterable principles that lie at the foundation of a person's attitudes, which in turn are the basis of their behavior.[127]

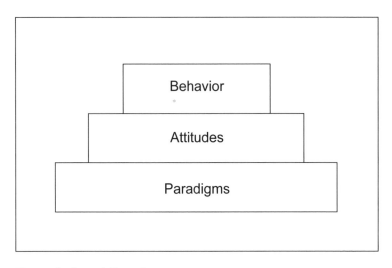

Figure 5: Covey's Paradigm

The paradigms and principles at the center of our life are the source of security, guidance, wisdom and power. A person who shifts from one principle to another experiences uncertainties and life becomes unstable. Ideally, one could create a single, well-defined center that generates a high degree of stability. Centering one's life on such a timeless unchangeable principle will result in a solid foundation for the creation of the major elements of character ethic.

Covey believes that once the correct paradigm is in place, one could develop habits that maximize efficiency. As an example, he describes a situation in which a man has invited his wife to a concert.[128] He has the tickets and they are ready to leave. At the last minute, his boss tells him that he has to attend an important meeting. His decision of whether or not to attend the meeting would depend on the principles guiding his life. If he is looking through a spouse-centered lens, he will go to the concert; if he is looking through a money-centered lens, he will stay at work in the hope that his wife would understand. If he was strongly influenced by his church, his decision might depend on other church members'decisions. Whatever his guiding principle may be, it will determine his decision.

If he is guided by character ethic, he would try to detach himself from the emotions of the situation and look at the whole picture. Whatever choice he makes, the important point would be that he consciously makes a knowledgeable decision and feels confident about it. Other people or situations would not influence his decision; it would only be guided by his own wisdom. His guiding principles would enable him to see things differently, to think differently, and to act differently. Using the correct paradigm, he would have a high degree of security, guidance, wisdom and power that flow from a solid unchanging core.

Assessment of Principle-Centered Leadership

The significance of recent leadership theories is that they challenge the paradigm of an outside-in or with-out approach, and start with the individual and promote inside-out or with-in concepts. However, they fail to address questions such as: What is the cause of such a fundamental change in a person's paradigm? What causes a person to see differently, to think differently, and to act differently? What is the source of empowerment and strength that enables individuals to overcome existing attachments, habits and desires? What is the ultimate factor that transforms their vision? What pulls them away from the webs that they themselves or the environment have woven?

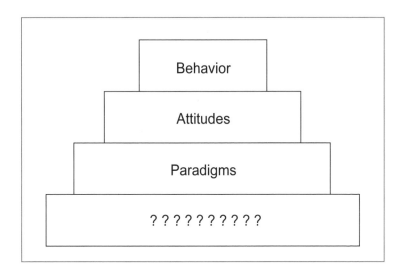

Figure 6: Bases of Paradigms

There are many people with a very strong character ethic, but they are unhappy and discontent with their lives. They are not empowered, and suffer from emptiness, stress, fatigue and lack of purpose and meaning. Character ethic is necessary but it is not sufficient to provide a solid foundation for prosperity and effectiveness.

As mentioned above, Covey distinguishes between character ethic and personality ethic. He explains that personality ethic is not original, but reflects artificial and false values imposed by society. Such values merely provide quick fixes and short-term solutions. He demonstrates the difference between character ethic and personality ethic in the form of a metaphor: If we consider a tree, its roots represent character ethic and the branches represent personality ethic. Since the roots are the foundation and the origin of the branches, one should direct one's attention to the roots.

Figure 7: Character and Personality Ethics

What is missing in the above picture is the true origin of the tree, the seed. Covey focuses on the roots and the branches, and overlooks the seed. It is necessary to recognize the fundamental role of the seed in the life of the tree, not just its roots and branches. Many people with a strong character ethic, who value fairness, human dignity and honesty, are still not content or empowered. The mere recognition of these principles does not help them make their lives balanced and tranquil. The lack of balance clearly indicates the absence of a stable center.

The real source of the tree's life does not lie in its roots or in its branches; it is the seed, which, under proper conditions and care, sprouts and grows in two directions. In harmony and balance, from that central point the roots grow into the earth, and the stem grows toward the sky.

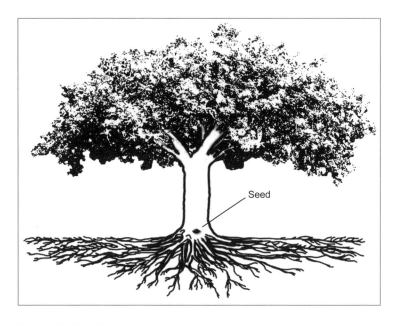

Figure 8: The Origin

The seed carries within it the tree's potential for growth and development. Its development represents the unfolding of what exists within it already. It is the blossoming of its potentials. The destiny of a tree is encapsulated in the seed. Therefore, if one believes that the roots, or character ethic, are the source of life, empowerment, and vitality, one misses their true origin.

A person with a strong character ethic is similar to a barren plot of land ready to be cultivated. The land is necessary, but cannot bear crops without seeds. In light of these deliberations, it is necessary to evaluate the fate of those who are honest, trustworthy and adhere to all social laws and regulations, but fail to recognize their value.

Character ethic and its principles are relative and changeable because they reflect the dominant norms and values of society. They change in different times and under different circumstances. Compliance with character ethic does not necessarily reflect the innermost reality of the human being. Why, then, do people conform to character ethic? Is it because laws, social standards, or codes of behavior enforce it? Or is it because of personal weakness, or powerlessness to challenge existing standards?

Man's position in society closely resembles the situation in a zoo. By putting them behind bars and wires, zoos artificially protect certain animal species that otherwise would be destroyed by predators. However, such measures hardly provide a lasting solution, since as soon as the bars are removed, the predators will again attack these species. Artificial social standards and codes of behavior prevent man from openly expressing his aggressive traits. Compliance with character ethic is based on artificial codes and unreal laws and standards, and only makes human beings suppress their natural instincts. Man becomes the captive of social norms, and is condemned to lead a life similar to that of plants and animals.

As natural organisms, human beings are a mass of cells that act according to outside stimulation in order to fulfill needs and desires. Many of these characteristics also occur in the animal world. However, in their complexity, human endeavors to satisfy needs and desires to the optimum transcend the reflexes of animals. Nevertheless, their constant attempts to improve living conditions reflect a deep-seated natural reflex.

Like other organisms, human beings follow the natural laws of absorption, assimilation, accumulation, and repulsion. But unlike most animals, they are unable to establish true balance of existence. Because of their greed and excessive desires, they tend to abuse and destroy personal and social relationships. Unable to openly express these aggressive traits, they set out to destroy themselves. As a result, they suffer from social diseases, such as depression, fatigue, stress-related illnesses, alcoholism, and drug abuse. In brief, they have to cope with the whole gamut of self-destructive forms of behavior.

Although human beings act and live in the natural world, their essence exists in a separate, elevated realm. They are exposed to changing outside conditions, but their essence remains constant. In everyday life, this eternal dimension remains hidden within them, and inaccessible to their reach. They cannot discover themselves unless they realize this hidden, eternal essence of being. While the laws of physics provide a certain degree of stability, the recognition of man's unchangeable essence produces timeless and universal laws.

Review of the evolution of Management Theory reveals that, to date, none of the major theories of management and leadership have provided a satisfactory and practical solution to the problems facing management. However, it is evident that the human factor is the most critical element to the success of the organization.

Before developing a solution to these issues, the chapters that immediately follow demonstrate that the shortcomings of political organization and sociology are similar to those in management.

2. Politics and Government

Throughout history, political leaders have experimented with a variety of ways to rule their subjects. Political organization, a study as old as mankind, has resulted in the specialization of tasks. Ancient man discovered that one could more efficiently dominate nature if individuals specialized in tasks in which they excelled. The transition from hunter-gatherer society to the establishment of agricultural village communities, to the formation of city-states and, finally, the creation of empires, was the logical outcome of this division of tasks.

As the number of individuals within society multiplied, coordinating their activities became increasingly difficult. Rigid social hierarchies developed with a political leader at the top, supported by an administrative elite and the military. The rest of the population had to support the administrative apparatus by paying taxes. The ruling elite in turn ensured their safety from external aggression and tried to minimize internal conflicts by enacting laws and regulations. This protection has remained the function of politics throughout history, although the manifestations of political organization and management have undergone significant transformations.

Often, irreconcilable differences have ensued between the interests of the ruling elite and the general population. Revolts, insurrections, and revolutions frequently challenged the existing order because the people were dissatisfied with the way their society was managed. During the last 5,000 years, there has been a gradual widening of political participation. While, in ancient empires and in Medieval Europe, one individual (an emperor or a king) owned the state and its population, beginning in the 18th century there was an evolution toward including a wider strata of the population in the political decision-making process. Those who met certain property, educational, racial, and gender requirements were permitted to vote. In spite of these advances, the question remained whether modern political systems really benefited each individual as they claim.

Political systems can be divided into empires, authoritarian systems, socialist systems, and democracies. It would be wrong to assume that they were developed on a historical continuum. Although today there is a strong trend toward democratization on a global scale, the outcome is far from inevitable; authoritarian systems coexist with socialist systems and democracies. Furthermore, each type of government appears in different manifestations and variations depending on its social and historical context. Each has its advantages and disadvantages and uses different methods to organize the individuals who form its constituent elements. All four types of political systems will be discussed in turn by presenting a number of case studies.

2.1. Empires

Empires are the most general types of political organization. They are usually dominated by an imperial administration that shows little concern for the affairs of its provinces except for collecting taxes. The further one moves from the capital city, the more limited the power of the central administration becomes. A small circle of bureaucrats and a strong military supports a ruler, who often legitimizes his power in religious terms. Empires are by nature multi-ethnic, but often only one ethnicity dominates the central administration, which makes no pretense of representing the interests of the majority of the population.

The **Abbasid Empire** (749-1258) was typical of this form of political rule. Headed by a Caliph, who claimed to be the successor of the Prophet Mohammad, the empire encompassed the modern Middle East and North Africa. After the Abbasids rose to power, they left the administrative structure of their predecessors unchanged. Local administrators ruled the provinces; they collected taxes from the subjects, but otherwise interfered little in their everyday affairs. The distance between rulers and subjects remained huge and followed the ancient Persian notion of kingship.

Each individual's role was predetermined by birth. Because of the Caliph divine legitimacy, individuals had no right to challenge his authority. They had to acquiesce to his decisions and those of his administration. Individuals belonged to certain ethnic, religious, and professional groups, each pursuing their own interests. The role of the state was merely to regulate the relations between these groups, and to ensure the harmony of society as a whole:

The world is a garden; its fence is a ruler or a dynasty; the ruler is supported by soldiers; the soldiers are maintained by money; the money is acquired from the subjects; the subjects are protected by justice; and justice is maintained by the ruler.[129]

The only unifying factor was the Caliph Islamic legitimacy. As long as the tax burden remained light, the population was uninterested in the central state. Ultimately, this lack of cohesion led to the disintegration of the Abbasid

Empire, as local potentates successfully challenged central authority. The Ottoman Empire, successor to the Abbasid, operated in a similar fashion and disintegrated for similar reasons during World War I. Nevertheless, the remarkable longevity of these empires is something to behold. Both lasted for over 500 years.

In conclusion, empires are primarily interested in preventing various ethnic and religious groups from challenging the central authority. Cases in which empires try to homogenize their population into a single culture are extremely rare. Empires by nature do little to accommodate the interests of all their subjects, but pursue a policy of *laissez-faire* as long as the stability of the provinces and the tax flow from the provinces to the center remain unchallenged.

2.2. Authoritarian Systems

Like empires, a small ruling elite dominate authoritarian regimes. The majority of the population is excluded from the administration and decision-making process. As the ruling elite's only interest lies in perpetuating its own power, such regimes permit independent development of different sectors of society, in particular, the economic sector. Following the definition given by the political scientist Juan Linz, authoritarian regimes are "political systems with limited, non-responsible political pluralism, without extensive or intensive political mobilization, and in which a leader or, occasionally, a small group exercises power within formally ill-defined but actually quite predictable limits".[130]

Authoritarian regimes occur in a number of manifestations. The ruling elite can be the military, a state bureaucracy, a party or other institution, religious leaders or groupings, class coalitions such as a land-owning oligarchy, or an industrial, commercial and transnational bourgeoisie. The legitimizing ideology ranges from national identity to "law and order", national security, revolutionary doctrine (Marxism), and ethnic declarations of solidarity (Arab socialism, Négritude).[131] Among the most common forms of authoritarian regimes are oligarchical regimes and theocratic autocracies. The following case studies of Nigeria and Saudi Arabia will elucidate the way authoritarian regimes function.

2.2.1. Oligarchical Regimes

These appear predominantly in Latin American and African countries. Military and civilian governments tend to alternate. Either the military seizes power from civilian rulers whom it considers corrupt, or civilian rulers call for the military to restore law and order. **Nigeria** is an excellent case study of the oligarchical type of regime. With over 140 million inhabitants and about 250 different ethnic and linguistic groups, Nigeria is Africa's most populous and diverse nation. Different military regimes, supported by a corrupt bureaucracy, have ruled the country for all but approximately twelve years (1960-66 and 1979-83), when civilians were in power.

Nigeria is an oil rich country. Were it not for continued mismanagement and malappropriation of resources by the government, every citizen would benefit enormously from this wealth. However, Nigerian politicians are notorious for their inclination to abuse their office to increase their personal wealth. Most politicians come from the prosperous business elite or they are leaders of ethnic communities. Since their main concern is their individual aggrandizement, they have done little to unify the country. In the words of one observer, "for the political elite, power was an end in itself and not a means to the realization of some greater good for the community".[132]

Under civilian rule, Nigeria had a multi-party system but parties were divided along ethnic lines. Election fraud ran rampant, and elections contributed little to the democratization of the society. The individual remained steeped in a web of ethnic and localistic forces. The state bureaucracy contributed further to excluding the majority from politics and had "been particularly effective in blocking or dividing pressures and incipient demands on the part of the rural and urban poor".[133]

The results of this regime are continued shortcomings in essential services such as water, electricity or the maintenance of law and order.[134] Numerous attempts to change this situation have failed. Despite its claims to end corruption, the military has never systematically interfered in the affairs of the bureaucracy. Noted political scientist Peter Koehn suggests that the problem of poor performance in the public sector will not be solved by purges, forced retirements, and privatization. Deeper structural and attitudinal constraints need to be addressed.[135] Unfortunately, there is little hope for more popular participation.[136] Without the empowerment of the masses, "public servants will continue to act primarily as self-serving agents of underdevelopment".[137] The only group outside the government bureaucracy and the military that has any significant influence in the political decision-making process is the so-called *Kaduna Mafia*, whose members are mostly wealthy businessmen or retired military officers.

As a result of the government's ineffective role, Nigeria has squandered its oil wealth. The bulk of petroleum money was spent on unproductive prestige-enhancing projects or it has ended up in the coffers of corrupt individuals, while it contributed next to nothing to improve the situation of the masses. Oil prices collapsed in the 1980s and the lopsided development of the previous decade was revealed. In 1989, Nigeria's national income was only 20 percent of what it was in 1980. Virtually all of the country's agricultural projects had been neglected and the country depended almost completely on the import of commodities. In order to feed its population, Nigeria had to seek outside assistance.

In sum, the combination of military rule and an inefficient and corrupt bureaucracy effectively exclude the masses from politics. The existence of political parties, a parliamentary system with a constitution, a president, a senate, and a house of representatives contribute relatively little to prevent widespread impoverishment. Politics in Nigeria primarily serves as a vehicle for the enrichment of a small number of ethnic, military, and bureaucratic leaders.

2.2.2. Theocratic Autocracies

Theocratic Autocracies do not have any political parties. The leadership, which can be a religious group or a single monarch, derives its legitimacy from religious tenets. Personal freedom and property protection are largely ensured as long as individuals do not openly contradict the ruling faction.

Since its foundation in the mid-18th century, **Saudi Arabia** has based its legitimacy on Islam. Another lasting feature of the kingdom is the significance of personal ties in politics, government, and business, rather than the principle of equal opportunity. Only recently has emphasis been put on an individual's education and qualification for government positions. Officially, there are no special interest groups.

Since the royal family bases its legitimacy on Islam, they claim to govern in the name of the people, the overwhelming majority of whom are Sunni Muslims. However, with the expansion of the educational system and the increasing sophistication of large segments of society, there has been increasing criticism of the royal family. The most vocal opposition comes from religious groups, who criticize the royal family for misrepresenting the true values of religion.

The kingdom does not have a constitution since it bases its legitimacy on the Qur'an and the *shari'ah* (religious law). Popular representation happens almost exclusively on the level of the *majlis*, an old Bedouin tradition where every individual has the opportunity to personally present a grievance to the king. The *majlis* is held on several levels by the king, the crown prince, senior princes, and other leaders of the aristocracy. Saudi analysts praise this system as being more personal than elections:

In Saudi eyes, the opportunity to speak personally to their rulers is more valuable than an occasional impersonal vote in an election, and makes elected legislatures unnecessary. The majlis is the place for the individual citizen to express his personal views, eliminating the need for political parties or labor unions. Nor is a free press considered necessary if every individual has the opportunity to talk directly to the king or to the king's representative.[138]

King Fahd himself declared after the Gulf War that "the democratic system prevailing in the West does not suit us in this region [...]. The system of free election is not part of Islamic ideology".[139]

The king's power appears almost unlimited. He is Prime Minister, Commander-in-Chief of the armed forces, and final Court of Appeal. He appoints all ministers, senior government officials, provincial governors, ambassadors, and high-ranking military officers. A crown prince, who is the heir to the throne, assists him as Deputy Prime Minister. The only limitation to the king's power is religious law. He also has to balance the demands of influential members of the royal family. Inside information into the decision-making process is unavailable.

The king conducts day-to-day affairs in the diwan, where he is assisted by advisors of domestic and international affairs. Occasionally, the king convenes a *majlis al-shurah*, an informal gathering of high government officials, to work out solutions to pressing problems. Because of these limited consultative institutions, some Saudi scholars rather euphemistically refer to the Saudi monarchy as a "consensus monarchy".[140]

The Saudi political system only works because the kingdom has distributed its enormous oil wealth relatively evenly among its citizens. Nevertheless, criticism of the royal family's excesses has been mounting in recent years. The less affluent citizens of the kingdom have become the main victims of the recent decline in oil prices.[141]

The continued lack of popular participation in the decision making process is now beginning to stir the economically disadvantaged strata as well as the country's *Shi'a* community, which traditionally has been marginalized. In short, authoritarian systems operate for the benefit of a small ruling elite and exclude the majority of the population. Economic wealth may mitigate demands for popular participation temporarily, but this type of regime in the long run is unable to provide for the well-being of all its citizens.

2.3. Socialist/Communist Systems

The number of Socialist/Communist countries has significantly declined after the disintegration of the Soviet Union in 1989. Nevertheless, this form of government provides an interesting example of how political rulers tried and ultimately failed to represent the well-being of the people. Socialist/Communist systems appeared in various manifestations, but all shared the following features:

- The working people, led by the working class, held the reins of power.

- The socialist revolution established the "dictatorship of the proletariat". Under "developed socialism" all working people organize under the banner of the dictatorship of the proletariat.

- The Communist party guides society and politics. It derives its mandate from the truths of Marxism-Leninism.

- The population is increasingly integrated into the political decision-making process through membership in work collectives and public organizations.

– State and society constantly have to be alert with regard to possible attacks by the "class enemy".[142]

In theory, Socialism/Communism aims to overcome the exploitation of one class by another. The ultimate goal is the establishment of a "workers' paradise". The theoreticians of Socialism/Communism maintain that individuals would liberate themselves from the shackles of the capitalist mode of production and achieve a state of harmony and balance if they follow the program of the Communist party. In reality, these regimes have failed to fulfill such lofty aspirations. A closer look at the former Soviet Union and China will demonstrate the reality of Socialist/Communist regimes.

The former **Soviet Union** was the successor state of the Russian Empire, but it never overcame the tradition of centralized power and absolutist rule. As one observer noted, "The Communist party can be viewed as a modern counterpart to the Russian tsars and emperors, who in their claim to total power ruled on the basis of divine right".[143] The Communist party dominated the Soviet Union. The party represented the entire population because it claimed to have access to the correct interpretation of Marxism-Leninism. The party infiltrated the political, social, and economic systems through over 400,000 so-called "primary party organizations", which could be found in factories, business enterprises, educational institutions, military units, and embassies.

There were general elections to the Supreme Soviet every five years. However, unlike Western democracies, in the Soviet Union elections served not to choose the most popular candidates, but to confirm those candidates already chosen by the Communist party. Another function of the elections was to demonstrate the people's loyalty to the party. Approval ratings of 99.9 percent or higher for party candidates were not uncommon.[144]

The Communist party organized the country in a strictly hierarchical manner. Underneath the decision-making organs (the Central Committee, the *Politburo*, the Secretariate of the Central Committee, and the Congress of the Communist Party), over 50,000 elected Soviets and various other organizations closely linked to the party infiltrated every aspect of society to ensure the population's loyalty.

Although Marxist-Leninist ideology called for the abolition of all ethnic and national differences, ethnic Russians who often controlled the affairs of the non-Russian republics dominated the country. At times, Russification programs caused much resentment in the republics. In this aspect, the Soviet Union differed from classical empires with which it shared many common features such as its multi-ethnic and multi-national composition.

The military played a dominant role in the Soviet Union, not only as a deterrent against the threat from the West, but also as an instrument to keep a dissatisfied population at bay. Opposition to the Communist party rule was systematically suppressed with many opponents ending up in prison or fleeing to the West.

Soviet leaders frequently claimed that their country's economic production would soon surpass that of the capitalist West. Except for the military sector, however, the Soviet economy remained backward. Popular dissatisfaction with inferior goods led to a "second economy" that produced higher quality goods with material obtained in questionable ways. Heavy subsidies of food, rents, public transportation and other public needs led to an imbalanced economy. Due to the absence of a money market, capital was often wasted. Inferior goods frequently ended up in warehouses because consumers refused to buy them.

In sum, the Soviet Union failed to implement its promises of providing maximum benefits for all of its citizens. Noted scholar Zbigniew Brzezinski lucidly summarized the situation:

"The Soviet society has acquired the wherewithal for further growth, and the bureaucratic and dogmatic restraints imposed on it by the ruling party have become dysfunctional to that growth. Thus the gap is opening between the society and the Soviet political system, in some ways reminiscent of the late Tsarist period. This condition is aggravated by a decline in the quality of the Soviet political elite, and by the growing assertiveness of various other key groups. The political elite, increasingly bureaucratized, self-centered, and aging, is unable to respond effectively either through terror or reform. The result is stagnation-which unless corrected by major institutional reforms, will lead to disintegration."[145]

China is the only Socialist/Communist superpower remaining in the world. Its political organization resembles that of the former Soviet Union in that the Communist party and its affiliated organizations dominate the country's affairs. China's political system perpetuates a strong historical division between rulers and subjects. For many thousands of years, the majority of the population had little contact with the government except at tax collection time.

Their beliefs were strongly influenced by folk religion, Taoism, Buddhism, and Confucianism.

Taoism emphasized the need to repress conflicts with known persons. The group, be it the family, the neighborhood, or the guild, played a dominant role. Individualism in the modern sense did not exist. Every person had his or her predetermined role in life and tended to act passively in the face of authority.

Confucianism sanctioned the outward compliance with authority, thereby contradicting the spirit of a modern political system that relied on the free exchange of opinions. Mao Tse-tung realized the debilitating effect of such a tradition, condemning "double-dealers who were outwardly compliant but inwardly unsubmissive, say one thing and mean another, speak in honeyed words to people's faces but play tricks behind their backs".[146] There were a number of major agrarian revolts, but the majority failed and never provided impetus for social change.

The majority of China's population was largely apolitical and the educated elite had a well-developed understanding of the political process. Most significantly, they had secularized the system in that they adhered to the traditional "Mandate of Heaven", which stipulated that rulers could be deposed if they violated their divine mandate. In addition, the educated elite had developed an elaborate system of recruiting the administration through highly selective civil service exams, stressing qualification rather than heritage.

In recent years, some remarkable changes in China's economic administration have come about. The economy was administered by the State until the 1987 Party Congress.

This congress initiated a gradual process of liberalization and an opening toward a free market. The Chinese leadership justified this move by embracing the theory that China was still in the first half of the century-long "primary stage of socialism" and that only after the completion of this stage would communal ownership dominate.[147] Intended to increase the prosperity of the people, the liberalization of the market entailed a number of negative side effects, including the layoff of millions of workers, high inflation, and a growing gap between the rich and the poor.

Personal freedoms remain subordinate to state ideology. With the exception of the constitutional period from 1954-1957, personal rights have become subject to the need of creating a socialist state. The opposition is imprisoned or has to flee into exile. A criminal code put into effect after Mao's death is applied in an erratic fashion.

It is certainly correct to ascertain that today Communist ideology is less important than it was in the past. One observer even maintains that China is no longer a Communist country in any meaningful sense.[148] Even if this is true, China remains an authoritarian, strictly hierarchically - ordered country, where the chasm between individual citizens and the ruling elite remains unusually deep.[149] The recent economic liberalization has done little to alleviate this situation.

In summary, Socialist/Communist regimes have been unable to implement the tenets of Marxism-Leninism, which promise that, under the leadership of the Communist party, every individual would overcome the exploitation of the ruling capitalist class. Instead of creating a "workers' paradise", they established strictly hierarchical political systems based on coercion and political conformity. Dissenting voices have been systematically persecuted. Instead of giving freedom to the majority of the population, the only beneficiaries are party officials and the military. Economic mismanagement further contributes to the division between political rulers, who appropriate scarce resources for themselves, and the population, which has to be content with inferior products.

2.4. Democratic Systems

The democratic type of government offers the general population a higher degree of political participation than empires, authoritarian systems, and Socialist/Communist governments. Universal and free elections are the main instrument for public participation in the decision-making process. Most democracies also safeguard personal freedoms, human rights, and free economic activities. Democracies certainly constitute a major advantage over other systems of government, but they are far from perfect. Criticism usually relates to the degree of state intervention, political apathy, the unequal distribution of economic resources, and the dominance of some classes over others.

2.4.1. Western Democratic Systems

In the West, democratic systems appear in different manifestations. The major distinctions are between majoritan, pluralist, mixed, and corporatist forms of government. Majoritan democracies have a one-party ruling cabinet and a two-party political system. The two political parties mainly differ in their socio-economic policy. This form of government adheres to the principle of representative democracy, in which government officials are elected to represent their constituency.[150]

Great Britain is one of the best examples of Majoritan democracy. Headed by a monarch, whose role is merely ceremonial, Britain's government consists of a cabinet whose members are from the ruling party. Strict party discipline in the House of Commons ensures the smooth operation of government in the hands of the majority party. Elections to the House of Commons are held every five years and follow the principle of territoriality; that is, the party with the most votes in each of the 650 electoral districts sends one representative to the House. This has resulted in a two-party system with the government alternating between Labour and Conservatives. Other parties have no chance to form the government, although they have sometimes carried over 20 percent of the popular vote. The powers of the House of Lords, which consists of 1,200 hereditary members, have been rescinded during the last decades and today it only has the power to delay legislation.

Britain has an elaborate welfare system, encompassing social security, the national health service, and personal social services. Since these services are financed by tax money, it has become increasingly difficult to maintain them. Pressures are mounting to partially reduce the services of the welfare state.

The British political system has been subject to severe criticism for its exclusivist two-party system and the inability of political institutions to respond to social change. The "policy of fragmentation persists in spite of the centralizing trends of the 1980s".[151] Compared to other European countries, state intervention has been minimal. "As a result the British governments have been poorly equipped to engage in the kind of highly positive interventions followed by most other governments in the European community."[152]

The political institutions of Great Britain today are virtually the same as they were almost a century ago. One observer deplores "[...] the incapacity of [...] the British political system to adapt to social changes [...]."[153] Another critic puts it more bluntly: "In the early 1990s we have, with the special exception of local government, much the same set of political institutions as before, operating in substantially the same way they did seventy years ago."[154]

The British bureaucracy lacks cohesion and the will to implement its politics. "The administrative style of British government has always been to entrust the implementation of most politics to other people-local notables, local authorities, and in some policy areas, interest groups. British government is formally and constitutionally highly unified. In reality, it is substantially fragmented."[155] The situation of the cabinet reflects the situation of the bureaucracy. Although highly centralized, it is internally fragmented.[156]

British governments receive their share of criticism for their "obsessive secrecy and their desire to manipulate information to their own advantage, which undermines Parliament's role as a forum for informed criticism and constructive debate. Together with the majority party's (i.e., the government's) control over procedures of legislation, they may deprive ordinary Members of Parliament of any real political influence at all".[157]

The record of the party system is more ambiguous. On one hand, it has been effective as an instrument of government, providing durable and cohesive administrations. On the other hand, it has failed as an instrument of popular representation. "As an instrument of representation, the party system is less successful. By under-representing the Liberal Democrats, Greens and, to a lesser extent the Scottish Nationalists, it keeps important issue areas such as the constitution, individual rights, and the environment off the agenda either permanently or too long. [...] Elections have become little more than referendums on the outgoing governments' recent economic record. [...] The party system does not carry out its integrative functions either across groups or between citizens effectively, to the disadvantage of effective government in the long turn."[158]

In the end, these deficiencies could have far-reaching consequences. "It may well be, indeed, that the pressures from change coming from European integration, Scottish, Welsh and Irish nationalism, disadvantaged groups and regions may necessitate change. Increasingly assertive and independent workers and customers cannot be accommodated within the existing constitutional structure."[159]

The **United States** does not precisely fit the model of majoritan government, since a one-party cabinet such as Great Britain's has more often been the exception than the rule. However, like Britain, the U.S. has a two-party system. Some analysts call the U.S. political system a pluralist democracy. A pluralist democracy is a society "dominated by powerful organized groups, and the government serves essentially as a broker, or referee, among them and also frequently participates as an interest group itself." [160] This model emphasizes self-interest as the guiding principle in politics. In pluralist systems, the majority of the population is content with the status quo and often shows political apathy.

The U.S. Legislature is divided between the Senate and the House of Representatives (the Congress), both of which are elected by popular vote, enjoy equal status and power, and are intended to balance each other. Passage of a law requires the approval of both bodies. Party discipline is weak, and members of Congress often give priority to their constituencies at the expense of the policy their party follows. One important feature of Congress is the committee system. Committee work serves the division of labor and allows for a higher degree of specialization. The majority party in each house selects all chairmen and always has a majority of their party sit on all committees.

Like Britain, the United States employs a two-party system. However, American parties are mainly vehicles to win elections. Unlike European parties, American parties do not present a well-defined ideology to their electorate. Their decentralized status and regional peculiarities often blur the dividing lines between their agendas. One of the issues haunting the electoral process since the mid-20th century is the skyrocketing cost of elections. Candidates have to be either independently wealthy or rely on donations from outside sponsors. Attempts to curb the influx of outside money have so far failed. Voter turnout has declined over the years. In presidential elections, hardly more than 50 percent of all eligible voters go to the polls.

U.S. interest groups fulfill functions similar to those of European political parties. Most interest groups represent business interests and are organized on a local level. In general, corporate interests exert the most influence, such as the oil lobby, the tobacco lobby, the dairy lobby and the sugar lobby. Some lobbies originate in the government itself, such as the military lobby. Government subsidies, or tax breaks for business, are the main result of these lobbies. Critics of this system argue that interest group politics counteract the principle of democracy and advocate stricter state control of these groups.

The territorial structure of the U.S. government is a compromise between the unitary form with a dominating central government (as it exists in France), and the confederate form, with near autonomy of its subdivisions. The U.S. federal system permits the existence of strong states with powers independent of the central government (police, taxation, education, health, and welfare), and a strong national government with powers that the states cannot claim (coining money, declaring war, foreign policy and commerce). Each state has its own constitution, its own government, and its own laws, all of which must be consistent with the U.S. Constitution.

Criticism of the shortcomings of the U.S. political system abounds. Scholar Samuel Huntington targets interest groups, arguing that, contrary to the claims of pluralist theoreticians, interest groups are the result of political apathy, not of a widely-shared consensus.[161] Congress has been criticized for being out of touch with the population. According to Lawrence Dodd, Congress is dominated by technocrats who pursue their own interests, not the interests of the people.[162] A perennial problem in U.S. Government is the role of the central government in relation to state governments. An ever-increasing central bureaucracy is often singled out as one of the major evils of the American political system.[163]

Finally, it is necessary to examine the influence of big business on politics. According to some analysts, there is a collision of interests between business and politics, which in effect excludes the general population from the decision-making process. "[...] One is struck by how the diffusion of power has led to undemocratic results and how the power of money has preempted the power of the electorate."[164]

Mixed Forms

Mixed forms of democratic government are more common than the few cases of consensual democracies, as they exist in Switzerland and the Libyan Arab *Jamahariyya*.

France represents the tradition of a strong intrusive government coupled with a multi-party system. France developed a centralized administration in order to overcome strong regional, linguistic, and class divisions. Until recently, successive regimes have established a network of state agencies throughout the country. Since the 1890s, France has tried to disperse a uniform political culture by establishing a centralized educational system which imparts knowledge based on enlightenment values, especially Voltaire, to the country's youth.

France's multi-party system is highly fragmented. Parties are divided into Left (Communists), Center-Left (Socialists), Center (Gaullists, *Union pour la Démocratie Française*), and Right (*Front National*). During the 1960s, the Gaullist party dominated, but declined in the 1970s. After 1981, the Socialist Party became the dominant force in French politics. It appears that France is moving toward a more consolidated multi-party system. One has to note, however, that there are strong forces both to the left and the right. While the Communists have experienced a steady decline, the Front National under Le Pen has scored some remarkable successes in recent elections. Participation in

French elections is high; it regularly exceeds 80 percent of eligible voters.

One of the most peculiar - and probably the most undemocratic-aspects of the French political system is the role of the civil service. The French civil service includes over 2 million persons. It is hierarchically organized and extends its structure deeply into the provincial administrations, thereby granting it the power to intervene in local government politics. A small number of the traditional and prestigious *Grand Corps* run the civil service. These groups include the Inspectorate of Finance, the Council of State, the Prefectoral Corps, and the Corps of Mines. The *Grand Corps* are tightly knit entities with their own characteristics distinguishing them from each other.

The *Grand Corps* recruit their members from a number of elite schools, such as the *École Polytechnique* (technical), the *École Nationale d'Administration*, or the *École Normale Supérieure* (teachers). Competition for admission is tough, and entrance exams are rigorous. Only the best graduates are admitted to the *Grand Corps*, while the rest occupy lower ranks in the administration. Members of the *Grand Corps* remain within their organization for a few years, and then transfer to other public bodies. In addition, many become managers in the private sector. Thus, the civil service exerts considerable influence on both administration and the economy. Inspectorates, administrative courts, and ministerial cabinets, all of which have relatively limited impact, perform control of the civil service.

Criticism of the French political system follows Alexis de Tocqueville's (1805-1859) observations that France was a country torn between the tyranny of the majority and autocratic rule.[165] Michael Crozier, for example, criticizes the strength of the central administration over popular participation. In particular, he blames popular culture for its over-reliance on central administration. Since the French are predisposed to avoid face-to-face conflict, they depend on the central administration to mediate conflict, but, because of their belief in enlightenment ideals, they resent the administration at the same time.[166] France is "over-institutionalized", with a top-heavy administrative system, which by far exceeds the demands of society. Inefficient and unresponsive institutions impede the functioning of a democratic government.[167]

Yet another variation of democratic systems can be found in **Scandinavia**; in Denmark, Norway, and Sweden. All have organized what political scientists call corporate pluralism. Under this form of government, Scandinavian countries differ from other democracies in their remarkable stability of political institutions, their democratic tradition free from military intervention, their emphasis on consensus building and cooperation rather than conflict, and the relatively equal distribution of national resources.

The Scandinavian countries use proportional representation rather than a plurality voting system. The objective of proportionality, a form introduced earlier this century, is to prevent the rising working class from gaining the majority. Instead of radical change, this system reflects incremental changes in the electorate as they happen. In addition, it ensures government stability.

Another interesting feature of corporate pluralism is the fast integration of immigrants into Scandinavian societies. Since 1976, foreign nationals in Sweden have been permitted to vote and run for office in local and regional elections after only three years of residence. Norway and Denmark have similar legislation. All in all, "Scandinavians rank extremely high on a wide variety of gauges of participation, for example, voting, party membership, organizational activities, signing petitions, participating in demonstrations, and contacting officials".[168]

In addition to parties, interest groups play an important role in Scandinavian politics. Membership is high (90 percent of the populations in Denmark and Sweden, 70 percent in Norway) and encompasses all strata of the public, including farmers, industrial and white collar workers.

These groups play a vital role in the political life of Scandinavian countries; an organized group covers virtually every aspect of human activity. Furthermore, interest groups are highly centralized.

Under the so-called "remiss" system, ministries are obliged to consult interest groups affected by decisions pertinent to that group. They are also represented on committees, which use policy-making proposals. Representatives from interest groups sit on the same boards as government officials and parliamentarians. Interest groups enjoy an extremely high degree of autonomy since they have the power to regulate, administer and police their own affairs. There are special labor courts to regulate conflicts between employers and employees without the interference of the state. As a result of the autonomy of interest groups, it is unlikely that the government will alienate its citizens.

Another vehicle for establishing consensus are standing and special legislative committees, which include members of the ruling party and of the opposition. The impact of the opposition on governmental actions is therefore considerable. It is possible to argue that the term opposition itself may be misleading in a governmental system that permits such extensive access to various organized groups, bureaucratic agencies, and non-governmental parties.[169] One of the major shortcomings of this system of consensus and compromise is that its operation can be exceedingly slow.

The most distinctive feature in Scandinavia is that of the welfare state. State services range from medical care and free education to social work agencies for the rehabilitation of the sick, the elderly, and the handicapped. There can be no doubt about the benefits of such services, but there are also a number of drawbacks. Taxation of the individual is very high, often amounting to more than 50 percent. Many companies have problems finding qualified workers, as workers tend to immigrate to other countries with lower tax rates. Finally, it has become increasingly difficult to raise the funds needed to run the welfare state, especially in times of economic recession.

While the Scandinavian political systems have received ample praise for their inclusiveness and stability,[170] there are distinct "neo-totalitarian" tendencies. In his study of Swedish politics and society, Roland Huntford criticizes the overpowering state and its stifling bureaucracy, which suppress individual initiative. The bureaucracy and business form a technocratic oligarchy, dominating the citizens in a dense network of rules and regulations. "Politicians have lost their significance in Sweden, supplanted by a form of technocratic oligarchy, which is apparently unassailable, because its tenets are universally accepted."[171]

"Modern Sweden has fulfilled Huxley's specifications for the new totalitarianism. A centralized administration rules people who love their servitude, so that technology may be efficiently exploited. Mentality has been guided to follow change and avoid conflict. It has all been achieved with means known to the West. Nothing that the Swedes have done is, in itself, original; their originality lies in their application. Personality has been suppressed, the collective worshiped at the expense of the individual. Given the European ethos, this might be expected to arouse rebellion, but not among the Swedes. They love their servitude. [...] Sweden is a control experiment on an isolated and sterilized subject. Pioneers in the new totalitarianism, the Swedes are a warning of what probably lies in store for the rest of us, unless we take care to resist control and centralization, and unless we remember that politics are not to be delegated, but are the concern of the individual. The new totalitarians, dealing in persuasion and manipulation, must be more efficient than the old, who depended upon force."[172]

2.4.2. Non-Western Democracies

A number of non-Western countries have adopted the formal principles of Western democracy. The results have often been peculiar crossovers between traditional forms of government and representative democracies. The list of newly emerging democracies is endless, particularly in the now independent states of the former Soviet Union. Since it is too early to evaluate their experiments with democratization, the following summary will confine itself to two countries that have introduced democracy, briefly after World War II.

In many respects it would be wrong to classify present-day **Japan** as a non-Western country because of its status as an important industrial power. However, Japan's political system remained in a semi-feudal condition until the country's defeat in World War II, and even today shows features of an incomplete adaptation of Western democracy, characteristic for Third World democracies.

Like Britain and the Scandinavian countries, Japan has a ruler, an emperor, whose function today is entirely ceremonial; he is, based on the constitution of 1947, a "symbol of the State and the unity of the people".[173] The Japanese Parliament consists of an upper house (the House of Councillors) and a lower house called the House of Representatives and it is elected by popular vote. According to Theodore McNelly, the "function of the House of Councillors is an enigma. If the House of Representatives is a truly democratic body and accurately represents the people's will, there is no need - from a democratic point of view - for a second chamber, which at best would only confirm the will of the democratic lower chamber and at worst obstruct the democratic will".[174]

After the war, the Americans wanted to establish a unicameral parliament since Japan did not have a federal political system. But the Japanese insisted on an upper house as a check to the lower house. As long as the upper house was not under the control of the opposition, the majority party in the lower house could negotiate legislation with the opposition. An upper house dominated by the opposition might obstruct any successful legislation.

Japan still does not have a federal government, but the country is centrally administered and has a number of elected prefectural governors, mayors, and assemblymen. However, they depend closely on the national diet, and cannot enact laws contradicting those passed by the national government. The local governments often lack funds to implement infrastructural measures such as roads and sewage lines.

To a large extent, Japan's decision-making process depends on behind-the-scene actions. Personal networks are an integral part of this process. On the positive side, this opens additional channels and provides more flexibility in difficult situations. On the negative side, the process depends on personalities rather than on formalized institutions, and can be excruciatingly slow because every decision is presented to a number of individuals.

"In Japan, informal channels are widely used to help the ruling party and government bureaucracy apparatus coordinate different interests in preparing politics. Through these informal and non-legislative means, it is relatively easy for the Japanese to reach a consensus among themselves, whereas in the United States, highly publicized political debates and a powerful legislative branch have made some highly sensitive policy issues more visible."[175]

Since the system depends on entrenched bureaucratic elite and functionaries, there are certain authoritarian features visible in Japanese politics. "Since 1947, despite its adoption of a formally democratic constitution and the subsequent development of a genuinely open political culture, Japan seems to have retained many 'soft authoritarian' features in its governmental institutions: an extremely strong and unsupervised state administration, single-party rule for more than three decades, and a set of economic priorities that seems unattainable under the political pluralism during such a long period."[176]

Japanese politicians frequently work, not for the benefit of their electorate, but only for themselves. As a result, the political apparatus becomes ossified and averse to innovations. " Leaders not only lack essential training, they have been formed essentially as followers and those who showed some signs of genuine ability may well have been discarded. Groups are increasingly afraid to entrust their fate to strong heads. [...] Having waited so long to rise to a position of authority, the ultimate heirs are usually out of touch with present needs and realities."[177] The political elite is unreceptive to innovation, and tends to dilute any new ideas into a conformist vision of politics.[178] "Politicians proudly make speeches which revel in a bright today and more brilliant tomorrow, only tacitly admitting difficulties by stressing how they will quickly be taken care of."[179]

An entrenched elite and a well-functioning state apparatus yield an ossified political system that has no ability to adapt to change. "The system is too solid and the elite too well in control to permit the adjustments which are necessary to adapt to major changes in the surrounding environment. [...] Instead of offering hope to those who are not pleased with the situation, it makes them assume that no possible improvement can be obtained from the political machinery."[180] The majority of the population has become disillusioned with the political process and abstains from participation in politics altogether.

More than Japan, **India** is rooted in traditional politics, although the country adopted a democratic system in 1949 after gaining its independence from Britain. Like Britain, parties and interest groups represent the people of India, but there are a number of significant differences. India's parliamentary system had to adapt itself to the country's heterogeneity that includes over 800 languages and dialects, a rigid caste system, and the predominance of small villages. Moreover, a considerable segment of the traditional Hindu community rejects secularism and parliamentary representation altogether. Another segment rejects these institutions because it adheres to communist ideology.

Unlike Britain, there is very little consensus about the usefulness of India's political system. Moreover, the social cleavages within Indian society are much deeper than in the West. A minute Westernized elite tends to defend the status quo, while the majority of the population lives in dire poverty. As a result, the proclivity to violence is high in spite of Gandhi's advocacy of non-violent resistance.

The Indian party system reflects the struggle between modern ideologies (capitalism, socialism, liberalism, communism) and traditional values. The major parties are known for their instability. For example, in the 1970s the Congress Party and the Janata Party split due to ideological differences.

Parliament consists of the Lower House, which is elected by popular vote, and the Upper House, whose members are mostly elected by state legislatures. India's legislative process is almost exactly the same as that of Britain. The Lower House has a system of standing committees that deal with all aspects of government operations. Parliament's main function is not political decision-making, but providing a forum for debate between government and opposition.

The president of India enjoys extraordinary powers, such as the dissolution of Parliament and the declaration of state of emergency. He is also Commander in Chief of the Armed Forces and is responsible for the appointment of state governors and Supreme Court judges.

The highest ranks of the bureaucracy are the most efficient elements in India's government. This is the direct consequence of a long tradition of British colonialism. Based on the British civil service, the Indian Administrative Service (IAS) attracts highly qualified candidates through a system of rigorous examinations and interviews. However, this applies only to the highest positions; middle and lower ranking officials often lack the necessary qualifications.

In spite of attempts to alleviate the enormous differences between rich and poor, progress has been slow. It is true that there is a growing middle class, but the number of impoverished individuals continues to rise.

India's political system has been criticized for the "tyranny of the bureaucracy" and the obstructive behavior of the opposition parties.[181] Some observers caution that over the years India's democratic process has eroded. The constitution itself favors security over democracy, providing for emergency powers to supersede democratic freedoms. What India needs is more political and economic decentralization, and more power in the hand of local governments.[182] Other points of criticism are the notorious corruption of politicians and the instability of the party system, which makes any meaningful democratic process impossible. Most importantly, it appears that the electorate has so far failed to internalize the democratic process and remains steeped in traditional patterns of behavior.[183]

Democratic political systems offer significantly more possibilities to the individual than empires, authoritarian, and Socialist/Communist systems. Nevertheless, they fall short of accommodating everybody's needs and desires. The party system is only an incomplete tool to diffuse existing tensions among various groups, and general elections frequently fail to attract the interests of the electorate because they believe that their vote makes little difference. Powerful economic interests often neutralize the democratic process and leave the people with the impression that political decisions have little significance for their lives and that politicians are interested more in their personal gain than in representing their constituencies' interests. Democratic systems, therefore, only offer superficial solutions to most problems of the individual citizen.

3. The Sociological View of Man and Society

Sociology studies the structure of society and analyzes the behavior of its members. Sociology also examines social change and tries to explain why societies accept change. The review of major theories of sociology can be beneficial in different ways, in that it enables individuals to analyze their own behavior and to examine the origins and causes of their conduct. By studying one's own behavior, one realizes that the so-called rational or obvious norms of behavior that most people follow rest on weak foundations. Most social norms and codes of behavior are based on customs and cultural values that have been passed on from generation to generation. In most cases, they are devoid of rational or objective foundations.

In this sense, sociology can help us understand the underlying aspects of social life. However, this endeavour can be quite unsettling. "Understanding the familiar in a new way is not always a pleasant experience. Very often we are startled to learn that the beliefs we have held onto for so long are not really true."[184] In most situations, people uncritically follow the customs and habits of their society. If we review the major sociological perspectives, we will realize how we perceive the nature of society, the nature of the individual, and the mechanism by which society functions. This realization will help us better understand our own actions and the way we respond to change.

3.1. Review of major Sociological Perspectives

Sociological theories can be divided into classical and modern approaches. Before discussing the difference between the two approaches we need to examine their main differences in terms of the nature of human beings, the nature of society, and the functioning of society.[185]

3.1.1. The Nature of Human Beings

One school of thought considers human nature as passive, morally neutral, and controlled by social factors. In this view, society creates the individual through forces "that are external to the individual and culturally created".[186] Among the major socializing agents are the educational systems, the family, and peer groups. They have coercive power and compel the individual to behave in accordance with social norms. In brief, individuals are the products of their societies.

The second approach regards human nature as good, cooperative, and decent, but holds the conditions of daily life responsible for making people act in evil ways. Therefore, "the solutions to social problems are to be found in the social environment rather than in individual fault".[187]

Finally, there are theorists who see human nature as rational and decisive. In this perspective, rational behavior is an action specifically calculated to attain particular goals. In modern society, traditional and emotional bases of action are replaced increasingly by rational and calculated action.[188] This rationalization process involves the specification and enforcement of rules and roles with a view toward efficient, predictable goal achievement. As a result, informal and customary understanding give way to formal, contractual relationships.

3.1.2. The Nature of Society

There are two ways to describe the nature of society. Those who regard it as independent of its members maintain that society as a whole is more than the sum of its individual members; society shapes the personality and consciousness of its members more than individuals shape the character of society. The nature of society is active and independent, and controls individuals' behavior. On the opposite end of the spectrum are those who insist that the whole of society equals the sum of its parts, or individual members, and that the dominant institution determines the nature of society. In Capitalism, for example, the dominant institution is the economic system.

3.1.3. The Functioning of Society

With regard to the mechanisms that make society work, the different assumptions are:

- The division of labor and the cooperation necessary to maintain it enable the society to function.

- There are permanent conflicts among different social groups. Through the use of power, society creates balance among the conflicting parties. In Capitalism, this happens through exploitation, and the conflict among interest groups.

- Society functions through accommodation of its members. The dominant system promotes voluntary cooperation.

3.2. Classical Theories of Sociology

The following brief overviews of three major proponents of the classical school of sociology will show how they perceived the three issues outlined above.

3.2.1. Émile Durkheim (1858-1917)

This French sociologist considered human nature as passive and controlled by society. In his view, individuals were morally neutral and society created their personality. Society existed independently of its individual members and it controlled individuals through social facts that are created by cultures, and it defined their way of thinking, feeling, and acting. The individual had little choice but to succumb to these forces. "It [was] not that one [chose] to go along with the prevailing social modes, it [was] simply that one [did] not realize there [was] a choice."[189]

In Durkheim's opinion, individuals learned the social facts from the educational and social environments, and because their nature was passive, society's norms and values controlled them. "In short, individuals [were] more the products of society than the creators of it."[190]

Since Durkheim believed that society existed independently of its individual members, he devoted his attention to examining groups and structures.[191] He believed that society worked because division of labor, and the fact that people needed each other to provide for their everyday necessities, facilitated individual cooperation. Cooperation, then, was the mechanism that made society work, and cooperation guaranteed its survival. He further claimed that when social facts lost their coercive power, social cohesion was achieved through solidarity.[192]

There are numerous problems with Durkheim's view of society. His assumption that human nature is passive, neutral, and totally controlled by society is reductionist. In his theory, human beings possess merely a materialist personality, which has very little to do with their true essence and identity. Another weakness of Durkheim's theory is his insistence that society has an identity independent of its individual members. This is very misleading because what would society be without its individual members? Individuals are the building blocks of society, and their true value, the common essence that each human being possesses, is the cohesive force that binds people together, leads to cooperation, and constitutes society.

3.2.2. Karl Marx (1818-1883)

Marx maintained that human nature was good and honest, and that it was not the source of conflict. Rather, it was the social structure that led to imbalance and injustice. The nature of society, from Marx' point of view, was determined by the dominating institution. The mechanism that accounted for the continuation of society was conflict of interest among different groups. Marx claimed that unequal distribution of power was the cause of social conflict because it allowed those in power to exploit the rest of society. Those who owned the means of production exploited workers. They became increasingly alienated and developed class-consciousness. They also realized that the system of exploitation would change only through violent resistance against the oppressors. Revolution, therefore, became "a vital necessity in the evolutionary process of society, [and] social conflict [was] at the core of society, the source of all social changes".[193] The goal of revolutionary social change was to create equality in the distribution of power and to reverse the exploitation of one class by the other.

Marx absolved the individual from any responsibility for social injustice. Instead, he blamed oppressive social structures for perpetuating exploitation and inequality. It was the system, or the social structure, which produced poverty, injustice, and conflict. "Therefore, the solutions to social problems [were] to be found in the social environment rather than in individual faults."[194] Moreover, he regarded social classes as the main culprits for sustaining the social system, and "placed great value on the group identifications and associations that influenced an individual's place in society".[195]

By giving priority to the role of the social system, Marx's theory underestimated the crucial role of the individual.[196] Like Durkheim, he considered individuals as inactive and uncreative, unable to control their own destiny or establish social harmony, which remained the responsibility of the dominating institution. For Marx, the dominating forces were institutional relationships. Society continued to function not based on harmony, but because of continuous clashes of interests and conflicts. However, such a view denies human capabilities and the possibility of human beings living in harmony and balance.

3.2.3. Max Weber (1864-1920)

From Max Weber's point of view, human nature was rational. Human beings were rational, could set precise goals, and direct their behavior toward the attainment of those goals. According to Weber, the Industrial Revolution led to the development of rationality. He maintained that those who wielded power in society should use their influence to make people provide their voluntary support to the state. Moreover, a network of relations and interrelations among its members characterized society. It functioned through collective actions and accommodations.[197] Unlike Durkheim, who studied the nature of social facts, or Marx, who was primarily concerned with the social system and class conflict, Weber emphasized the importance of social action.[198] He stressed that human beings attach subjective meaning to their behavior. In brief, social action reflected their internalized values and motives.

In Weber's opinion, human beings were naturally good and decent. However, the nature of society could be either rational or irrational. The reasons for irrationality were traditional social norms and values that dominated societies for a long period of time. Increasing rationalism, in Weber's opinion, was the key to social change because it eroded irrational traditions. As a society grew more rational, its traditional authority was first replaced with charismatic authority, and finally with rational - legal authority.[199] In Weber's theory human beings were active agents whose ideas were significant in social life. They made choices and their decisions and reasoning were the base of their behavior and conduct. In other words, human beings had a rational nature.

However, Weber failed to provide a means to evaluate human rationality. How can we measure rationality? Human beings set goals based on changing social norms. But norms and values are unstable and are subject to constant change. Therefore, rationality within the limitations of time and space has no universal validity. The foundation of rationality in the Weberian sense rests on limited human perceptions within the boundaries imposed either by the social environment or by man himself.

3.3. Modern Theories of Sociology

3.3.1. Structural Functionalism

The American sociologist Talcott Parsons (1902-1979) is the most influential proponent of functional analysis.[200] This theory regards human nature as responsive to its social conditions. It perceives society as a self-regulating and self-maintaining social system, composed of many interrelated parts that are structured to maintain the stability of society. This theory emphasizes that society is a system that functions through actions and interactions of its members. Cooperation and coordination are the mechanisms through which society works.[201]

A major flaw in functional theory is that it sees people as responding to the requirements of their societies, trying to find their place within the social order. Once they have found it, they tend to stay in that place. If people change, they do so in the manner determined by society. Thus, to functionalists, society is the active agent in history, and human beings respond passively, and are little more than tools within their social context.[202] However, does not the prosperity of any society or organization depend on the cooperation and communication of its members who have to be active and motivated? This can only be achieved when individuals discover their values and potentials.

3.3.2. Symbolic Interactionism

George Herbert Mead (1913-1963) introduced this theory, which studies human interactions within one-to-one situations and small groups, to American sociology. Mead observed the most minute forms of communication (smiles, frowns, nodding, etc.) to understand their significance within the larger context of a group or society.[203] This theory views individuals as social, active, and communicative, and considers society as consisting of networks of interactions among groups and individuals. The proponents of this approach regard symbols as important components of human communication. They point out that human beings can interact with each other because they share the meaning of both verbal and nonverbal symbols.[204] In this theory, society continues to function because people are socialized to meet role expectations from the time of birth and because the interdependency of individuals makes them rely on each other for necessary services and rewards. Further, the internalization or the requirements of various roles motivates the person to wish to fulfill them, thus society works through cooperation in fulfilling expectations.[205]

Modern theories of sociology modify and refine classical theories. Both theories maintain that human nature is active and responsive. Structural Functionalism builds on Durkheim's theory. Modern Conflict theory is influenced by the work of Karl Marx, but emphasizes harmonious social relations rather than conflicting institutional relations. Symbolic Interactionism studies social relations, symbols, and artifacts.

Both classical and modern theories are limited in a number of ways. Macro approaches of social change reflect the view that society has an identity independent of its members. However, in reality, there is no such thing as an abstract social identity because the identity of the individuals who constitute society cannot be dissolved into something independent of them. An individual is not a political or an economic variable, but constitutes a true unit of existence. A reductionist perception of this reality leads to misrepresentations. If society constitutes a system consisting of individuals and their behavior, how can imperfect variables add up to a sound and efficient social system?

In order to overcome this flawed view of the human in society, we need to start on the micro level, and recognize the role of the individual. The reality of mankind is the cohesive force that bonds individuals, organizations, and society at large. Society functions based on the inherent common value of its members. When the limitations imposed by the dominating social norms are lifted, the human reality as a true unit of existence will emerge. This is the real mechanism, which facilitates the functioning of society.

4. Theory "I" - The Inner Dimension of Leadership

"Whatever exists and is constant and unchangeable is Truth."
Sadegh Angha[206]

The review of management, political organization, and sociology demonstrates that current theories fail to take into consideration the true value and potential of the individual. They maintain that the solution to existing problems has to start with changes on the macro level, not with the individual. Another point to bear in mind is that the suggestion of behavioral theories to satisfy the needs and desires of the individual remains extremely difficult due to the diversity and changing nature of such needs. As long as these theories analyze only actions and reactions, or stimulus and response, they remain superficial and unable to recognize the real needs and motives of human beings.

Current management theory maintains that a successful manager should recognize workers as unique individuals who respond to different motivations. The assumption is that the more managers know about motivational techniques, the more successful they will be. In other words, managers have to develop innumerable plans and methods to motivate a diverse workforce. This is impossible. To date, none of the major theories has provided a satisfactory solution to the problems facing management.

This chapter will introduce Theory "I", a theory that goes beyond the physical dimension of human beings into the unchangeable and eternal dimension and the inherent value and potentials hidden within each individual. By discovering their inner dimension, human beings will gain permanent knowledge and will be guided by eternal and infinite principles. This theory is based on the logic that the wise are those who gain benefits and avoid losses while the ignorant are unable to distinguish between their losses and benefits. In order to distinguish between right and wrong and between gain or loss for ourselves or society, we need a gauge that remains unaffected by place, time, or social conditions. For example, without standardized units to measure time, weight, or distance, it would be extremely difficult to have effective personal, social, economic, or political interactions.

What, then, is this unchangeable gauge that helps us discover the true value and potentials of the individual? What gauge would enable us to distinguish between right and wrong, to gain benefits and avoid loss? Time, place and all external conditions are changeable variables and therefore cannot be used to discover the stable and constant reality of human beings. One must move within. The following examples will elucidate this point:

Seasons change the outward appearance of nature. In spring, a tree represents life, but in winter, it embodies death. On the surface, nature goes through drastic changes, but beneath the surface, life continues in a constant and unchangeable manner. The physical composition of the human body changes constantly. New cells continuously replace old ones, and within a decade, almost all the body's cells are replaced by new ones. Similarly, human thoughts and opinions are in a constant state of flux, and many thoughts and opinions change as time passes. New experiences and circumstances make individuals change their points of view. Human relations are also very volatile.

Love and affection profoundly affect us, but sometimes change into enmity and disdain. In brief, fettered by the limitations of physical being and social conventions, human beings experience changes and uncertainties that prevent them from discovering balance and truth.

In order to discover the reality of the individual that exists independently of artificial rules and regulations, it is necessary to transcend existing boundaries and leave behind the sphere of action and reaction, social conduct, and the laws of physics. Human beings are confined by the limitations of space and time. From a superficial point of view, human existence is subject to constant change and instability, but in spite of this seeming state of flux, each individual represents a complex organism characterized by a high degree of stability, order, and balance. Life on earth could not have continued for so long unless the various dimensions of human beings were in an intricate and logical interrelationship with their internal and external environments. As it is subject to space and time, the physical body consists of a metabolism and precise cellular functions that have accounted for the survival of the human species for hundreds of thousands of years. Current research in the fields of physiology, biology, chemistry, physics, and astrophysics constantly discovers new aspects of relationships with the environment and the universe.

The endeavors of scientists to understand every minor aspect of the human organism give evidence that it is of utmost importance to fully comprehend the human being. The mechanisms and functions of this organism are so complex that one expert alone is unable to diagnose all its organs. Separate specialized branches and subspecialties of medicine have evolved to fully analyze the function of each organ.

Psychology and psychoanalysis also try to better understand human nature by investigating dimensions of thought and personality that are so far unknown. To achieve this goal, scholars study human behavior, individually and within their social context, and generalize their observations in theories. Until now, their research rests mainly on hypotheses based on the observation of actions and reactions, and neglects the human being's source of strength residing within.

Economics, political science, and social sciences define the individual as a social actor. According to such interpretations, individuals depend solely on material conditions because they act mainly as producers and consumers. Outwardly they seem to be in control of their fate when they create and execute the laws of society. In reality, they are subject to the same laws and the power structures they created for themselves.

In light of the shortcomings of the social and political sciences, psychology and economics, how can we reach a comprehensive understanding of human nature that includes both outward and hidden characteristics? The inner dimensions of human beings necessitate the creation of a stable social system. Any system that forces them into a rigid structure not in harmony with nature and their personality is bound to collapse sooner or later. Thus, only a system that is in harmony with human essence will be permanent.

For this reason, it is necessary to know the universal personality of human beings from the point of view of *Sufism*, a 1,400-year-old discipline that introduces each person individually to his or her own inherent values and true personality. It represents a method that reconciles individuals with their real value. It trains people to develop their creative abilities so that they may benefit from all the resources provided by nature, and gain access to the true source of contentment, productivity, satisfaction and empowerment.

The great Sufi Molana Hazrat Shah Maghsoud Sadegh Angha, states: "In nature's destination, the pacts of man are apparent, but to the senses, they are unknown."[207] Astronomers estimate that our solar system is many billions of years old. The age of the galaxies and of the entire universe is much greater. This observation is relevant because the inconceivably long age of the universe makes us wonder what accounts for its stability in spite of a multiplicity of changes and developments caused by such forces as motion and gravitation. During this inconceivably long time, the universe has remained in balance, although it continues to change and evolve. What are the laws that prevent disorder in the universe and govern all its entities and their interrelationship? Do the planets of the solar system not revolve around the Sun, and are their distances from the sun and each other not determined by the forces of gravity and motion? Do the same forces that govern the planets and galaxies not exist within every atom?

In short, the balance existing among the planets and galaxies has ensured the stability of the universe over billions of years, notwithstanding all the changes it has experienced. Like the universe, forces that ensure stability and balance govern humanity. The following section will explore the forces that account for this high degree of stability. They are the principles essential to true leadership.

4.1. The Fundamental Principles of Theory "I"

4.1.1. The Principle of the Prevalent, Informed Center

Permanent balance and equilibrium is the result of every single unit following the guidance of its informed center. This principle applies to every aspect of nature, be it a single cell to the human body or the entire universe. The center is stable and constant and remains unaffected by changing conditions in nature or life. In Theory "I" the individual is the ultimate source of empowerment and the origin of all actions. This theory attributes utmost importance to the human being. Individuals who follow the guidance of the stable center are in a state of equilibrium, in harmony with nature. As a result, they can tap into their unlimited source of wisdom, knowledge, and creativity and tackle all situations and problems.

There is a fundamental difference between the concept of the "i" and the true "I". The "i" is subject to changes and fluctuations. Only when the "i" is transformed into "I" is it possible to implement meaningful and lasting change. If human beings discover and recognize the stable center, the wisdom hidden within it will permeate every aspect of their being and influence all actions.

The "I" is like the seed of a tree, containing all its hidden potentials and determining its destiny. From this seed will grow the trunk, the bark, the roots, the branches, the leaves, the blossoms, and the fruits. But the seed will only grow if it exists within a proper environment and it receives appropriate care. Under such conditions, the seed will develop, and pass on its inherent energy to the trunk, the branches, the roots, and the leaves. The tree will grow in balance and harmony because it receives energy and direction from the seed at every stage of its development. The seed determines which minerals the roots have to absorb from the soil, or in which direction the tree should turn its branches and leaves.

The seed represents the "I", the true identity of man. Every individual has only one "I", a seed that needs to be cultivated. The purpose of Theory "I" is to discover the stable center and to facilitate the unfolding of human potential. The concept of the "I" is infinitely superior to the "i". The "i" reflects the expectations, values, and norms of society, and rests on personal and social boundaries, as well as rigid norms and standards. The true "I" exists independently of space and time and is immune to change. The "I" is the constant and unchangeable gauge to distinguish between right and wrong, to gain benefits, and to avoid losses.

When individuals discover their stable center and respond according to their innate wisdom, they will be in equilibrium. When they are at the center of their being then they will be able to see everything from all angles - from 360 degrees. By reaching this point they are free and no longer limited to imaginary boundaries. Theory "I" introduces each individual to his or her true identity. Only an organization whose individual members have recognized their true value and identity will be able to reach a state of optimal creativity and productivity. Only a society whose individual members have recognized their true value and identity can reach a stage of health, balance, and prosperity. The leaders of such a society will adhere to noble and universal laws, and each individual will develop a new vision of life beyond the confines of social rules and dominating paradigms.

4.1.2. The Principle of Equilibrium and Balance

"Equilibrium of absorptions is the point of freedom."
Nader Angha[208]

Equilibrium and balance constitute a true and genuine principle that governs every aspect of human existence. The physical nature of human beings exemplifies this principle. The human body is naturally in a state of balance. All organs of the body fulfill a specific function, each contributing its share to the system as a whole. The result is a healthy and balanced individual. Imbalance or disease occurs when this balance is upset, usually by an external agent such as a virus or bacteria, or by an individual's choice of lifestyle, such as an imbalanced diet or lack of exercise.

The Principle of Equilibrium and Balance governs every aspect of life, be it the microscopic world of atoms, the cells and organs of animate bodies, the human being with its energy and potentials, or the vast extents of the universe with its stars and galaxies. Such equilibrium is the consequence of a permanent and unchangeable center. In other words, what we observe in the universe also holds true for smaller units of the material world. In the solar system, each planet revolves around the sun in an orbit based on the central position of the sun, its own mass, and the position of the other planets. If equilibrium and balance govern the universe the same principles apply to its smaller units, from the atom to human societies, since they are parts of the universe. Each unit is subject to the same principles that govern every other unit, no matter how big or small it might be. In the case of the human body, equilibrium and balance entail permanent well-being and health. For example, the pH level (indicating acidity/alkalinity) must be balanced, kept within very limited boundaries or one's very life is endangered. If a person reacts strongly to severe or continuing stress, the body cannot regain homeostasis, the immune system is compromised, and the result is illness. The following diagram demonstrates this principle:

One Cell → Cells → Organ → System → Human Body

Figure 9a: Effects of Balance and Imbalance (The Person)

The same principle also applies to organizations, political formations, and social groups:

One Employee → Employees (Team) → Departments →

Organization

Figure 9b: Effects of Balance and Imbalance (The Employee and the Organization)

One Citizen → Citizens (Parties, Interest Groups →

Government → State

Figure 9c: Effects of Balance and Imbalance (The Citizen and the State)

If each individual is in balance and utilizes his or her innate creativity, wisdom, and knowledge, the whole organization or political group will be imbued with this spirit at every level. In such a situation the laws and regulations of an organization or a state will no longer be arbitrary, based on fears and constraints, but empowered and motivated employees and citizens will cooperate with an enlightened leadership. The same principles that govern living organisms and organizations also apply to society as a whole:

Individual → Group → Society → Societies → Mankind

Figure 10: The Individual and Mankind

This constant law that permeates both the universe and the atom, as well as human societies, has universal validity. By discovering the stable center, the true "I", as well as the unlimited dimensions of the human being, it is possible to transcend boundaries and follow the guidance of the stable center.

4.1.3. The Principle of Cooperation and Collaboration

"In the infinite world, because of its unity, contrasts and antagonisms cannot exist."
Sadegh Angha[209]

The discovery of the stable center leads to equilibrium, and ultimately to cooperation among individuals instead of competition and conflict. On the surface, life seems to be dominated by disorder and strife. Upon closer examination, however, it becomes obvious that there exists an underlying harmony. Scientists usually wonder why organizations compete with one another instead of cooperating. Professor Sadegh Angha states in *The Hidden Angles of Life* that if we put the questions differently, we might notice that in reality all organisms form part of a balanced whole.

Which cell or molecule can feed or struggle more than its living capability? Not one, otherwise it will upset its life equilibrium. The unity of existence does not allow us to know the being of beings deeply separated and isolated from each other. The appearance of a tree shows that branches and leaves are separated, but they follow their way of life in a common stalk because of the unity of existence, which leads these beings in their course of life.[210]

To put it differently, there is no competition in nature; its constituent elements form part of an integrated whole devoid of conflicts or antagonisms. Water, for example, appears in different manifestations as liquid, ice, or steam depending on external conditions. The same holds true for all matter. While it assumes different shapes in different situations, its composition remains the same. All molecules and cells remain part of the whole, and fulfill their functions to maintain equilibrium.

We tend to see all matter as being separate and isolated from everything else because our senses prevent us from recognizing the true unity of existence. We only see the separate branches and leaves of a tree although they depend on the roots for sustenance; roots, branches, and leaves form a harmonious entity. Similarly, the human being is part of the infinite universe. Everything is interdependent and sustained by the unifying force of existence. Our limited view makes us perceive contrasts and opposites, good and bad, light and darkness, beauty and ugliness, energy and matter. However, they are all manifestations of a single reality, and only appear different in relation to time and space.

The concept of good and evil, unity and separation, reality and imagination, etcetera, have all come into being due to our limited sensual faculties. Thus, our eyesight is limited, but vision unlimited.[211]

Cooperation and order are the foundations of this universal harmony. Often, the laws of nature and human actions seem random and arbitrary. However, if the laws are seen against the wider background of the whole of existence, they all constitute elements of an interrelated, meaningful whole. The human body represents such an orderly unit, characterized by the cooperation of its individual constituents. Every single cell fulfills its predetermined function. The cells of the eye, the cells of the bones, the cells of the heart, for example, operate independently from the others, and yet make their contribution to the functioning of the whole body. Therefore, the cooperation of all the body's constituent elements leads to equilibrium and health.

Every organization assigns to its members certain tasks. If all members were encouraged to fully utilize their own unique potentials, they would function at their best and contribute to the overall welfare of the organization. Each individual has his or her own unique potential that materializes in the form of different talents. A system functions most efficiently when each individual members' talents are fully utilized, and when all members cooperate for the benefit of the whole. Professor Sadegh Angha summarized this principle this way:

The local growth and display of various aspects of peculiarities of being is a manifestation of the immense wondrous and creative power of capability that individuals or society as a whole present in particular or in general, in a multitude of ways and even diverse manners. The creative and unchangeable capability that is hidden (within every being) fashions the growth of the plant - from branches to fruits - in such a way that the onlooker never mistakes one for the other.[212]

In other words, the plant's inherent capability permeates from the roots to the fruit. At each stage of the growth, its essence guides its development. On the surface, there appear to be contrasts and differences; the harshness of the roots seems to clash with the delicacy of the flowers' scent. However, when we look at the whole picture, we notice that every single part is in an intricate relationship with the whole.

The same contrasts and differences appear in an organization. Management and employees often seem to oppose each other, or short-term and long-term objectives appear to be in contradiction. However, when individuals are integrated within the structure of the organization and function according to their inherent capability and talent, such contrasts and differences cease to exist. The key to achieving such harmony is through gaining access to the stable center, the "I". The "I" prevents us from being misled by conflicting values and choices or from becoming influenced by greed, selfishness, or competition. It makes us realize that our contribution to the whole system is unique and valuable. It helps us understand that the performance and survival of the whole depends on the contribution of every single one of its members.

As a system, an organization resembles the human body. Every cell must function properly to enable the organs to perform their tasks and to contribute to the health and balance of the body. The same law applies to an organization where every member has to contribute to the welfare of the whole. Notions of relativism will not mislead persons who discover their inherent capabilities and value. They will use their true value as a reliable gauge to evaluate their own conduct, and to guide them in the right direction.

"According to logical reasoning discerning the reality of objects is not possible without knowing their ultimate value."[213] One of the main causes of inefficiency and ineffectiveness in a social formation or an organization is the members' ignorance of their inherent value and capability. As a result, human resources remain unutilized or underutilized, creating an atmosphere of competition, distrust, negativism, and insecurity, where individuals and leaders struggle only for their own interests, thus sacrificing the well-being of the whole.

The best plans, the latest technology, and the most innovative techniques are worthless unless they are implemented properly by fully utilizing all resources and assets available.

Human resources are the most valuable asset of any social, political, or economic unit. Cooperation, empowerment, and teamwork contribute to its success. If it wants to succeed, it must recognize the value of every human being. In the example of the tree, the seed contains all the information necessary for its future development, and the environment influences which of its inherent potentials come to fruition.

In the 21st century, leaders have to rely more heavily than before on human skills, apply them in an innovative way, and empower every individual. As long as schools impart the idea that the key to success is competition, such a transition is unlikely to happen. It is necessary to realize that racial, religious, and ethnic diversity represents the unity of human existence, and that diversity is a source for creativity, not for conflict.

4.1.4. The Principle of Comprehensiveness

The constituent elements of the "I", and its true essence, include stability, equilibrium, cooperation, order, harmony, and love, all of which apply to every aspect of an individual's life. The "I" is a stable center that brings all aspects of life into balance. When the "I" is discovered, cultivated, and developed, it permeates the entire human being, and influences all aspects of ones life, be it the physical, mental, emotional, or spiritual. This is the Principle of Comprehensiveness. If a person, for example, is dynamic and positive, he or she will use this asset in every situation and operate more effectively. This principle encompasses the whole universe, the unlimited wisdom of human existence, and all dimensions of life. In the example of the tree, the seed is the comprehensive center. It is the source of the tree's life and determines each stage of its growth.

Each stage hinges on the Principle of Comprehensiveness and the environment that facilitates the fruition of the seed's potentials. When human beings recognize their stable center - when they discover, cultivate, and develop the "I", - it will permeate all dimensions of their life. Acting from the stable center creates a balance between the physical, mental, emotional, social and spiritual aspects of life. These aspects are interrelated and interdependent, each affecting the other in determining total well-being.

Organizations strive to promote health among employees. Based on this principle, promoting health goes beyond treating symptoms and focuses on the roots of detrimental health habits. Apparently, awareness and knowledge of health-promoting behavior is necessary but not sufficient to produce the required action - for example, a physician who is aware of the hazards of smoking but continues to smoke. Does the physician really want to hurt himself or herself? Of course not, but he or she does not feel the motivation, strength, and control to get rid of the unhealthy habit. A person gains the necessary motivation, strength and control when he or she acts from the stable center. It will reconcile the various aspects of being, and provide harmony and unity.

Society can only prosper when every single member recognizes his or her true value. Such a society will follow the Principle of Comprehensiveness and experience equilibrium, harmony, and cooperation among its members. In an organization, the Principle of Comprehensiveness enables managers to expand their vision and to perform their tasks beyond the limitations of cultural and social factors. In brief, the Principle of Comprehensiveness means that individuals discover their common inherent value, and the common source of life, that pertains to each and every human being.

4.1.5. The Principle of Harmony

To achieve a state of harmony, individuals must first unlearn all the limiting customs and habits they have acquired throughout the years. They have to know their true identity and liberate themselves from all limitations imposed on them. Every individual enjoys a wide range of capabilities and talents but they cannot utilize them to their full extent because of outside limitations. Only when they discover their true value and potentials will they reach harmony with themselves and their environment. Human beings are part of Existence, and as such they are in harmony with it. However, outside limitations imposed on them prevent them from realizing this harmony. By transcending these limitations, they will again be in harmony with the whole existence.

It is often assumed that there exists a chasm between human beings and the universal truth, between matter and energy, and between human beings and the Creator. However, what appears as a chasm in reality is only the absence of harmony that renders the recognition of reality impossible.[214] Within the confines of such limitations, humanity cannot realize the eternal truth, which is inaccessible to the senses, and requires access to a higher level of consciousness as well as a higher concentration of human energies.

To grasp any concept that its mark on nature imprints, to develop and to expand up to it, dissolving all boundaries, an interaction has to evolve, a relationship well established, with love of, and dedication to, the knowledge involved. An infinite exchange is the very first condition, the very first hints, in this sublime process; sensual perception, with frail limits and worries, can never uncover and illuminate the reality, or herald its gist; sensual perception alone can merit no great discoveries or riddles solved.[215]

What human beings cannot perceive with their senses they tend to dismiss as non-existent. Lack of harmony prevents them from realizing the unlimited potentials of existence. The infinite will never become manifest as long as they accept the limitations imposed on them. The human body is naturally in harmony and balance. Each organ functions independently and yet works in harmony with the entire system for the welfare of the whole, which in turn ensures the survival of all its parts. Each organ represents an aspect of the eternal truth, but it does not represent the truth itself. Failure to acknowledge the difference between the eternal truth and its different manifestations would be tantamount to accepting the limitations imposed on humanity. Our physical and social limitations severely constrain our ability to recognize the unlimited truth, which lies beyond our physical senses.

The same principle applies to our senses, all of which have different capabilities, such as the ability to perceive light, sound, and scent. However, these perceptions are conditioned by the nature of our senses. In reality, light, sound, or heat consists of waves, which are a form of energy. Waves of different lengths and intensity stimulate different senses.[216] Certain long waves are perceived as heat, while some short waves appear as sound or others as light. These different manifestations of energy appeal to the compatibility of a particular sense with a particular wavelength. Energy remains the unchangeable essence of all senses and perceptions, but due to our limitations, we can only experience it partially, and in different manifestations.

Originally, human beings were in harmony with nature and capable of receiving what existence provided. However, by accepting the limitations of society, they voluntarily restricted their senses and energies, depriving them of the opportunity to experience their real essence. Their focus and energy became scattered, and each of their senses only perceives a fraction of the infinite.

To re-establish harmony, human beings must free themselves from the limitations of their senses, gather all their energies, and concentrate them in the center of their being. This endeavor resembles the act of moving a boulder that rolled off a mountain and blocks the way. To remove it, one needs to find the center of gravity and place a lever under this point. The lever's energy is then sufficient to move the boulder and reopen the path it had blocked.

For human beings to liberate themselves from all limitations and experience the infinite, they need to gather and concentrate all their energies in the stable center of being, the "I". The result of this effort will put them in harmony with themselves and their surroundings and they will experience eternity. They will appreciate the knowledge, the freedom, the vitality, and the dynamics of their lives. They will experience their true essence.

4.1.6. The Principle of Guidance

The Principle of Guidance differs from the above principles in that guidance is an individual matter. In society, individuals are members of numerous groups, such as the family, the neighborhood, and professional associations. These groups provide for their members' needs and ensure their survival. When individuals begin their search for self-knowledge and true identity, they tend to rely on those methods that are familiar to them. People often try to discover truth collectively, and rely on the same methods their predecessors used. However, blind reliance on tradition frequently leads them astray. One has to recall that each human being's potentials and talents flow from the same source of life, from Existence. Why, then, do they rely on traditions that are external to themselves when they strive to realize their internal potential and capability?

The Principle of Guidance is a remedy for such reliance on external traditions because it constitutes solely an individual effort. This quest for self-knowledge is a journey from the limited insights of the "i" to the realization of the true "I".

In order to accomplish this journey, human beings need to receive guidance from their stable center, and rest in a state of harmony, devoid of all limitations and boundaries imposed by society. By concentrating their energies, they will reach a higher level of consciousness, and become capable of receiving guidance from the inherent knowledge and wisdom, which is bestowed upon them.

Therefore, guidance or leadership cannot be acquired externally by following the examples of social groups. Leadership and guidance at the personal and organizational level is possible only through recognition of the "I", and the efforts of every individual. The reality of guidance, its energy and its empowerment emanate from the stable center, which functions as a compass. Like a compass, it always points in the right direction. Independent of external conditions, it remains constant and unchangeable, and it leads each individual toward perfect equilibrium.

The Principle of Guidance is not part of traditional political, sociological, and management theories, which support the idea that control should lead or motivate individuals. In reality, leadership and guidance are micro issues. Leaders should facilitate personal development, and personal transformation. In addition, they should pay attention to the establishment of educational centers that facilitate the development of each individual's internal capabilities.

In an organization, teams and different departments are assigned different functions and responsibilities. In each one of these departments, employees function according to their specialties and talents. If employees are motivated and empowered to give their best, the results can be astonishing. However, in most situations, this is not the case, and lack of motivation and cooperation results in low efficiency and productivity.

Personal empowerment and leadership are the outcome of the true source of leadership and guidance. Thus empowered, each member of an organization performs his or her tasks with commitment, passion, courage, and innovation. The same principle also applies to political parties and interest groups. If every member follows the Principle of Guidance, there will be cooperation and harmony, and as a result, increased prosperity.

4.1.7. The Principle of Love and Attraction

Most political and management theories concentrate on developing a strategy that can unite people through a spirit of cooperation and unity. To achieve this aim, these theories elaborate concepts such as shared vision, common responsibility, teamwork, corporate culture, and quality circles. In reality, however, the results have not been entirely satisfactory, because current methods work with a collective approach and devote their attention exclusively to the social context of the individual. They fail to provide lasting solutions to existing problems because they ignore the original source of all actions and reactions. In brief, these theories are in disharmony with the true nature of human beings, and merely provide short-term solutions.

The Principle of Love and Attraction transcends limited and changeable attachments, dependencies, and emotions. Love is a fundamental principle of existence, a field of attraction, and a rapture that embraces the entire human existence. All existence is love. Like other manifestations of existence, love has its own reality.

The ordinary level of love finds its expression in everyday life, sexuality, friendship, and attractions. People often mistake sexual passion and sensual sexuality for the real and ultimate form of love, when in reality it is the lowest form. The veils of the lower levels of love obscure the higher levels. In order to recognize the higher levels, the veils of the ordinary must be removed.

Ordinary love, which is a manifestation of divine love, has real traces of true love. The lives of those who are in love are full of meaning and purpose. They are positive, hopeful, passionate, and giving. They see beauty as more beautiful and problems as less severe. However, because ordinary love is changeable and unstable, these feelings can turn into the opposite.

Real love, the rapture that is hidden in the "I", is constant, and its positive characteristics are permanent and eternal. In ordinary love, there are expressions of hatred, evil and goodness, ugliness and beauty, suffering and pleasure. However, true love is an essence. It remains constant and does not change or fluctuate.

Professor Sadegh Angha describes love as synonymous with the most delicate and spiritual levels of life. Love is the power that binds together the particles of matter, and sculpts the manifestations of Existence into its multitudinous shapes. Love is the very glue of existence.

The reality of love is a burning essence, which is hidden within the core of each element and strives to reach the state of boundless unity to bind and unite with the all-pervading love of existence.[217]

An example from nature will aid in better understanding the Principle of Love and Attraction. A drop of water measures only three millimeters in diameter. When we enlarge it many times, we can go beyond the level of molecules and enter the realm of atoms. In the structure of one hydrogen atom, we notice that the electron, like a small fireball, is revolving around the central proton at an incredible speed. So a Lover, rapturous in love, with a burning heart, is centered on his Beloved and is completely absorbed by love.

In the oxygen atom, we also notice such an attraction and rapture. A single drop of water contains millions of such electricity centers and fields of attraction. The human body is 75 percent water; thus it is capable of being so attracted. All of existence is governed by the same Principle of Love and Attraction, from the realm of subatomic particles to the orbits of the planets that revolve around a stable center, the sun.

If human beings, who, like everything else are imbued with this principle, neglect their stable center, they can only experience love in its ordinary and limited dimensions; they will remain utterly unaware of the burning love and rapture which is the moving force of life. "Love is an all-pervading electromagnetic force, which unites and connects all aspects of the existence, from the smallest particle to the whole infinite universe."[218]

This attraction unites every aspect of existence; it connects human beings to their source of life, to their stable center, the "I". The "I" functions as a magnet that captures all energies, love and attractions that exist in the universe. All individuals have their stable center. When they discover and unfold it, they develop shared values and the ability to connect and bind together. It works like an invisible glue and leads them to develop patterns of cohesiveness, cooperation, attraction, and love in its true meaning. Individuals imbued with the Principle of Love and Attraction are dynamic, vital, hopeful, and positive. Wherever they are, their presence radiates positive energy and liveliness.

On the other hand, failure to discover the stable center results in contradictions, ruptures, and divisions. Failure to develop and cultivate the "I" and its principles, will let social, cultural, ethnic, gender, and racial forces pull each individual in a different direction.

It is impossible to create a common vision or establish organizational cohesiveness and true team spirit by focusing on surface phenomena or strengthening social relations. Only if we discover each individual's common value, which exists independently from the limitations of race, gender, ethnicity, etc., will the stable center of the "I" act as a magnet, which responds to the magnetic field of attraction. Cohesiveness and team spirit will occur naturally. In addition, every individual in an organization will be deeply attracted toward achieving the same goal and vision. This attraction occurs in the center of the "I", in the core of an individual's existence, and from there pervades the entire being until it finally emerges on the surface, and leads to team spirit, cohesiveness, cooperation, and unity.

In an organization, the fundamental principles of the "I" manifest as follows:

Prevalent, Informed Center*................................Creativity & Vision	
Equilibrium & Balance*...Stability	
Cooperation & Collaboration*......................Teamwork & Coherence	
Comprehensiveness*..Synergy	
Harmony*...Compatibility	
Guidance*..Innate Knowledge	

*These principles manifest (become a reality) only in the presence of the ultimate principle:

Love & Attraction

Figure 11: Manifestations of Principles

The following diagram demonstrates the fundamental principles of Theory "I".

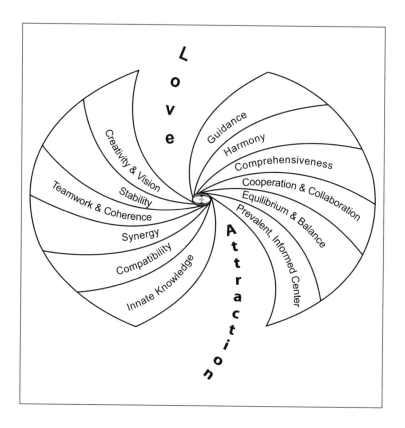

Figure 12: Fundamental Principles of Theory "I"

5. The Recognition and Discovery of "I"

Human beings fail to recognize their true nature, their reality, because they have imposed boundaries on themselves. As a result they are only aware of a limited dimension of their being and remain totally unaware of the vast inherent knowledge that existence has granted them. Sufism teaches that human reality far exceeds our common perceptions. Knowledge of Sufism helps us discover this reality.

While we tend to believe that science provides a picture of objective reality of "the world out there", quantum physics has forever crumbled that comfortable sense of reality. Scientists in other disciplines have also concluded that humanity's knowledge of reality remains shrouded and incomplete.

British physicist Paul Davies has written about the world we have learned to think we see and the absoluteness of existence. He stated that science is usually believed to be the basis for the construction of a picture of objective reality of the external and physical world. With the advent of quantum theory, this vision of reality has disintegrated and is being replaced by a revolutionary concept. Laboratory experiments have repeatedly demonstrated that atoms and subatomic particles, which are usually envisioned as miniscule little things, are not really things at all, not tiny separate specks of matter with a well-defined, independent existence, but active forms of energy.

Science is now demonstrating that reality is not a measurable property of the external world, but is instead intimately intertwined with our presence as observers and our own perception. Davies tells us that previous scientific "revolutions" had successively diminished the role of mankind from being the central player to a "mere spectator of the cosmic drama".[219] Quantum theory reinstates us, as observers, to the center of the stage, to the key role.

Another scientist who addressed the issue of absolute unity of existence was David Bohm, an American physicist who lived and worked in Britain and was also a colleague of Einstein. Bohm theorized what he called an "implicate reality" lying beyond the limits of our "explicit" senses. He said this "implicate order" included all particles and all electrons, including ourselves and the rest of the universe. While our limited senses see "things", with autonomous, separate existence, Bohm argued for a general law in which all objects and all times are folded together, a law where "everything implicates everything", in an order of undivided wholeness. This was a very different perception,[220] a new paradigm that contradicted the ordinary held conceptions of reality.

The benefits of this new view of reality and the order of the universe have unparalleled implications for humanity. For instance, neuroscientist Karl Pribram states, "for the first time in three hundred years, science is admitting spiritual values into its explorations. That's terribly important".[221] Bohm sees the very nature of the universe, of matter, of life and consciousness as projections of a common ground.[222]

Because humanity fails to perceive or cognize its true situation in existence, it also fails to understand the true meaning of spirituality, which is to know the truth of existence. To understand the reality of existence is to know the truth of one's constant self. The self is a tender and expansive essence that encompasses all things. The famous Swiss psychotherapist Carl Jung speculated about the "self", holding that it embraced the center of our totality. Jung went on to speculate about a major principle in Sufism. He said that the great spiritual leaders of humanity, the ones we call prophets, must be understood as role models to show us how to reach life's ultimate goal - self-discovery. Jung said that, "though we know of this self, yet it is not known", and then concluded that: "If the self could be experienced, it would be unlimited and endless. If I were one with self, I would have knowledge of everything."[223]

Discovery of the "I", the source of life, is the beginning of the journey toward self-knowledge. Sufism enables human beings to become aware of this eternal dimension within them and to recognize their unity and wholeness.

5.1. Sufism, the Way of Knowledge

Sufism is generally accepted as the mystical dimension of Islam. Although the origin of Sufism has been variously explained and interpreted, I would like to present it the way I have experienced it. Sufism is the reality of religion. By this I mean experiencing God in one's inner self, submitting to Him, and loving Him with one's mind, heart, and soul until no other but the beloved remains. This is the reality of religion, as I know it.

Although I was born and raised in a family where my great grandfather, grandfather and father had all been Masters of the Oveyssi School of Sufism, I was never allowed to think that because I was born and raised in the tradition, I knew it all. My father always said that spiritual learning and development was a matter of personal effort and discovery.

The Oveyssi School of Sufism dates back to the time of the Holy Prophet Mohammad and Imam Ali (peace be upon them). The founder of the school is Hazrat Oveys Gharani,[224] whose way of inward cognition was approved by the Holy Prophet. The inspired and revealed spiritual knowledge has been passed down from the time of Hazrat Oveys to myself through an unbroken succession of Masters who are well known by historians and scholars.

For 1,400 years, the Masters have taught students not to be followers, but to be masters of their lives. The word *irfan* captures the essence of Sufism. *Irfan* is derived from the word *ma'rifa*, which means cognition. In this context, it means self-knowledge that leads to knowing the reality of Existence and being replete with divine knowledge or mysteries. It is the way of prophets. This is why I have defined Sufism as the reality of religion. Sufism teaches that all knowledge is humanity's legacy, but one does not receive it until one truly seeks it. And until it is fully experienced in one's own lifetime the reality of the message of each prophet will never be known.

The quest for self-knowledge, for eternity, is universal. Those people for whom the quest for the ultimate Reality is the most important goal in life, and who do not give up their search until they discover the answer, are generally regarded as "mystics". Mysticism is associated with mystery and the unknown. It is a mystery to those who have not had the experience. However, for those people who have had the experience it is a reality. The mystical experience is usually associated with a sense of liberation, freedom, ecstasy, unity, contentment, abundance, compassion, knowledge, joy and love.

Throughout time, people have attempted to express the ineffable quality of the mystical unity of all existence. This underlying unity has been the message of all the religious traditions. External circumstances and ignorance, however, have caused the alienation and misunderstanding that has existed and still exists among religious followers. Existing cultural, geographical, economic and political matters have colored people's perception of God. Institutionalized religion must not be confused with the reality of religion. The reality of religion transcends these concepts. The point of divergence in all religious traditions takes place when the experience is formulated into words and images in the minds of those who have not had the experience themselves.

The point of convergence is the experience of the One Reality. Only the Reality within us can guide us to Reality; only when the transient becomes the Reality can one say: "I am Reality." It is through submission that the state of oneness and unity is attained. This means that the boundaries of individuation and limitation are demolished, and the individual as a true open system is in harmony with the whole existence. This is the state of total freedom and love that has been amplified in the writings of the Sufi masters. Physicist David Bohm's general law, described earlier, states that everything implicates everything. There is no existence but existence. There is no reality but reality.[225]

To know what a Sufi speaks about, one must experience the same. Sufism teaches that human beings are capable of discovering their eternal dimension that is hidden within them but is inaccessible to their limited comprehension. The goal of Sufism is the discovery of this dimension, and the recognition of every individual as a true unit.

William James, the founder of American psychology and philosophical pragmatism, stated that "our experiences are a function of what it is we agree to pay attention to".[226] To this the Sufi would add, with what faculties we attend, and how. Only by recognizing all dimensions of the human beings will their true value become apparent.

5.2. Dimensions of the Human Being

5.2.1. The Physical Dimension

On this level of existence, human beings, like other living organisms, follow the natural laws of absorption, assimilation, accumulation, and repulsion. But unlike most other creatures, they are unable to establish true balance because of their greed and uncontrollable desires. Human beings therefore tend to abuse and destroy natural resources and neglect personal and social relationships. In this dimension of existence, human beings are slaves to their insatiable needs and desires, which only lead to more needs and desires as soon as they have satisfied them. They seek peace and tranquility in the midst of instability. They try to find purpose and meaning for their lives. They want to fill the emptiness they feel. They strive to accumulate more, and to accomplish more in order to feel fulfilled and content. The more they try, the less satisfied they become. Eventually, they feel like robots whose function is to produce more, and to consume more. They create imbalance in themselves and in their surroundings and experience stress, greed, insecurity, fear, fatigue, and depression.

All these negative effects are the outcome of humans' failure to recognize their internal source of balance and tranquility, their true being. Living only in the dimension of matter and materialism results in deprivations and slavery. If human beings limit themselves to the shackles of desires and meaningless actions, they will never know their true identity and their innermost source of knowledge.

5.2.2. The Eternal Dimension

Just as precious diamonds do not deteriorate in the dirt of swamps, the veins of pure gold keep their luster within the heart of the earth and are loath to mix with the brittle soil. Human beings also bear a distinctive attribute in their earthly, natural existence, which is luminous and has a life of its own.

The eternal dimension lies hidden within human beings and is inaccessible to their limited perceptions, thoughts and senses. In this dimension, limitations and boundaries cease to exist and differences in race, ethnicity, culture and gender are insignificant. Instead, the true value of each individual, which is the common essence among all human beings, governs.

This dimension remains buried under the multiple layers of misteaching and limitations imposed by social norms and habits. It is not nourished and developed and has no manifestation. Therefore, when human beings encounter the concept of spirituality, they tend to deny its existence. The artificial distance between the "i" and the "I", between physical and spiritual dimensions, remains intact. As a result, human beings lose touch with reality in its unified form due to boundaries imposed on body and mind. To establish the lost harmony, to get back in touch with reality, human beings have only one choice: to return to their original source of life, to the "I", the point where being manifests itself in the form of matter.

The stable center of human beings, the "I" which acts as a gauge to measure and recognize the reality of the human, reflects the true laws of existence. The true laws of existence are constant and direct each phase of growth and development. Recognition of the truth of the individual in their eternal realm results in constant and reliable laws, and makes their existence more balanced. Thus their being becomes the source of knowledge and love. The ability to be firmly rooted in this constant dimension allows individuals to realize their true potentials and capabilities beyond the limitations of the physical dimension.

Spinoza, the 17th century philosopher, stated:

"The soul has the choice of uniting with the body, whose idea it is, or with God, without whom it cannot subsist or be conceived of. If it is united only with the body, it must die with the body. But if it unites with something that is immutable and enduring, it will necessarily endure with it."[227]

Prophet Mohammad (peace and blessing be upon him) has said: "Each human being is like a mine, gold, silver or jewel; excavate the goodness within them, so that you may have peace."[228] The Holy Prophet Jesus (peace be upon him) provided instructions on the importance of mining, of bringing forth, that which we have within us: "That which you have will save you, if you bring it forth from yourselves."[229] Sufism is the way to evolutionary development, to discovery of the precious treasure within.

Sufism teaches how human beings can discover their eternal dimension. It is often assumed that there is a chasm between the physical and the eternal dimensions of human beings. However, what appears as a chasm in reality is only the lack of harmony. Sufism re-establishes the lost harmony through proper education and development, and leads each individual to the discovery of himself/herself as a true unit of existence.

5.3. Education and Development

"Principles that are used in limitation are not the means for discovery of the infinite."
Sadegh Angha[230]

Contemporary sociological theories on education and development maintain that personality is a reflection of culture and that it has three main components:

- The cognitive component consists of thoughts, perceptions, and memories.

- The behavioral component includes talents, abilities, and skills.

- The emotional component encompasses feelings.

All three components of personality are learned during socialization, and one of the most important functions of socialization is the development of personality.[231]

Earlier theories investigated different aspects of education and development. One of the main issues revolved around the controversy of whether nature bestowed onto human beings certain inherent characteristics that constitute their personality, or whether it provided a nurturing environment that facilitates the development of personality through learning. Put differently, at birth, did babies already have the elements that constituted their personality, or was personality conditioned by what they learned during the span of their life? Sociologists agree that a combination of both factors account for the development of personality.

Today both the extreme theories have been rejected. Neither nature nor nurture completely determines the kind of person a human being will become. The biological and social factors each play a role in determining our personalities. On the other hand, we can learn only what the society has to teach us.[232]

The development of personality is one of the most important functions of socialization. Most sociological theories recognize these two functions of education: the transmission of values, attitudes, and behaviors from one generation to the next, and the transmission of knowledge and skills.[233]

Psychology differs from sociology in that it describes human development as "the study of age-related changes in human behavior during the life span".[234] Psychology primarily focuses on changes as they occur chronologically during the life of a person. On the other hand, psychology fails to tell us exactly how development and growth happen. Interestingly, the dictionary defines "develop" as to "unfold" or "unwrap", "expand", or "bring into activity". But Western psychology uses different definitions because it ignores the inherent education hidden within the human being; it defines education solely as a collection of acquired knowledge and limits it to the mere acquisition of information.

Sociology and psychology assume that human knowledge is acquired from the external world through the five physical senses. Likewise, learning is based on sensations and observations of external appearances, and focuses on " the study of behavior as it relates to perceiving, thinking, remembering, or problem solving".[235] In sociological and psychological theory, the goal of education is the development of human social character. An individual's character depends on external factors, such as social norms and values, culture, customs, and economic situations, not on inherent potentials or capabilities.

It is important to emphasize that education is generally considered as knowledge acquired from the social environment. The development of capabilities usually refers to the ability to communicate. In this sense, development is limited to an unfolding of human capabilities according to a biological timetable, and they come to fruition when a person reaches a certain stage of maturity. In brief, the study of human development primarily focuses on physical, mental, and social changes as they occur during a person's life. Sociology and psychology fail to tell us how to invoke the unfolding, the expansion, the growth, and the development of the ideal human being.

It is clear that the above theories on education and development have severe limitations because they assess character building on the basis of environmental factors only. They neglect the main question, which asks if human beings possess an inherent value whose recognition and development can lead to true knowledge. A related point to consider is whether or not human beings have inherent capabilities that they have been unable to discover because they use the wrong tools.

To understand these issues, we have to know the true self of every individual, detached from personal tastes and predilections, language, habits, geographical location, and all other human traits conditioned by nature and environment. When we know the gauge through which we can realize the true self we will be able to apply it to other systems as well. When we know the true value of one person, it is possible to discover other laws of action built upon these values. Such factors as economics, living conditions, social attitudes, and personal tastes are all peripheral to the main principle.

From the perspective of Sufism, education and development are not limited to environmental factors. In Sufism, education is an inherent and natural process that can easily be observed in every organization and structure and within each human being. For example, if we look at human hands, it becomes obvious that each muscle and nerve is directed and educated by an inherent knowledge to fulfill the functions of each hand. Nature provides this basic education regardless of our will, desire, tastes, thinking, or interference.

When children are born, they develop the education that is already implanted in their being. For example, when they develop their auditory system, or focus their eye muscles and lenses to distinguish objects and dimensions, they simply develop their existing educational faculties. Children who are in a state of balance inherently have the capability to speak. This is an education that is already implanted within them. The development of this education enables them to speak a particular language. If they fail to develop this inherent education, they will be unable to transform their innate capacity into speech.

The development of such inherent capabilities is not limited to biological aspects, but needs to happen in all dimensions of human existence. Unfortunately, most people are subject to incorrect teaching methods, which prevent the development of their capabilities and talents. Sufism provides the key to the discovery of inherent education, and facilitates its proper development.

5.3.1. The Recognition of Inherent Education and Its Development

To understand how the recognition of inherent education and its development influences the discovery of truth, we will study the senses and the limitations of the mind and the discovery of truth and the necessity of the concentration of energies for breaking boundaries and limitations.

Limitations of the Mind and Senses in the Discovery of Truth

Education from the perspective of Sufism does not consist of acquired, theoretical or experimental learning, but it is an inherent and natural process that can easily be observed in every human being. To elucidate this point, we need to analyze the human learning process, and the tools used to acquire in-depth knowledge.

In every situation, individuals use their senses to acquire and evaluate new information. However, it becomes obvious that there are limitations to the abilities of the brain and senses when it comes to the discovery of the unlimited Truth. What human beings call wisdom and rationality, and use to measure truth, is in fact only a limited view of reality, and has little to do with the Truth of universal wisdom and knowledge.

The ability of the brain to discover Truth is limited. The brain depends on information it receives through the senses. The natural limitations of the senses limit the brain's capacity. The human brain consists of millions of neurons, and each organ of the body has its own particular center in the brain. The information received by the senses is transferred through neurons by an electrochemical process. Through the patterns of electrochemical exchanges between neurons, the brain receives, analyses, and transmits all the information necessary to carry out its functions.

When the electrical impulses reach a particular center of the brain, they create electrochemical patterns. The brain compares and contrasts these patterns with the information, which is already stored in the memory, and as a result a person responds to a situation based on the interpretation of the information stored in the memory. For example, when we see a person in the street, our eyes pick up impressions, and send messages to the brain for interpretation. If we know that person, that is, if there is information about the person stored in our memory, we respond accordingly. Our brain functions much like a computer. It works according to pre-set programs, but cannot transcend these limits.

The structure of a computer is similar to the human brain, the senses, their organization and function. The basic principle for the assimilation of information consists of a precise and logical program that organizes, correlates, and compares the inputs with the given program, deciphering the inconsistencies from the numerous numbers and symbols. This simple mechanism with its fast and precise computational capabilities does not possess an innate intelligence to make decisions to analyze facts and figures, or to create and construct logical theories. Therefore, its input and output are first of all based on the given program and secondly, on limited inputs.[236]

In other words, the programs that a programmer has written limit the scope of a computer's function. Computers have no innate intelligence. The human brain functions the same way. Whenever we face a new idea or an unknown subject, this information is processed in our mind just as someone presses a key on the keyboard of a computer. The brain then compares this new entry with the information already stored in the memory. Based on this information, we accept or reject a new idea. This process is usually called "thinking". Therefore, acceptance or rejection of new ideas is based on limited information gathered through the senses, and the information stored in the memory.

As mentioned above, the brain functions according to a pre-set program and cannot go beyond that. Input and output change with the addition of new information. It interacts with a continuously changing environment. Since Truth is constant and unchangeable, it is clear that the infinite cannot be known through the limited perceptions of the senses and the brain.

The brain's output depends on physical inputs. If the given inputs are incorrect, its output is also incorrect. For example, we know that our senses are limited because they can only receive the waves that are within a certain wavelength. We cannot perceive the light waves or the sound vibrations with a frequency or wavelength above or below a certain level. Our ears can only hear the sound vibrations between 16 and 16,000 hertz. Similarly, our eyes can only see a limited part of the spectrum of light waves; infrared light or radioactivity is inaccessible to our senses, even though they can be measured with technical tools.

Human knowledge is based on information gathered by our physical senses.It helps us form an image of reality but it is not reality itself. Reality must be received, not perceived. Perception is based only on the brain's comparison of what has been previously recorded in the memory. It is the brain's translation of information provided to it by the physical senses. Given these limitations, we have to ask ourselves if it is possible to discover the universal truth through relying on the narrow perceptions of our senses. Hazrat Shah Maghsoud Sadegh Angha succinctly summarized this idea when he stated: "Principles that are used in limitation are not the means for the discovery of the infinite."[237]

To recognize the constant and unchangeable essence of the human being, to discover the reality of the "I" one must venture beyond the limitations of the senses. Of course, one needs to use the tools that are in harmony with existence. As mentioned earlier, we do not see with our eyes alone, but rather with our eyes and brain together. The impressions from the outside world create an electrical stimulus that activates a particular center of the cortex, such as the brain's principal vision centers. The brain compares the electrochemical patterns with the data and patterns already recorded in the memory.

In other words, seeing becomes possible through the activation of the primary visual cortex and other specialized places in the brain that make sense of visual data. If one replaces the impressions transmitted to the brain with internally generated electromagnetic impulses, the same results will emerge. Current research shows that:

If your primary visual cortex were entirely removed or destroyed, you would be blind. To turn the situation around, suppose that your brain was normal while your eyes were blind, or were simply closed. And suppose electrical stimulations were applied to the visual areas of your brain. What happened would vary with the part of brain that was stimulated. You might see flashes of light, colors, stars, etc.[238]

The brain is unable to discover Truth by itself because it relies on the limited capacity of the senses. Sufism instructs humanity that "things are not as they seem", because we pay attention only to the surface of things with our senses and scattered energy. We know, for instance, from the sensory sciences, that the eyes see only a tiny fraction of the vast energy that engulfs us. Aldous Huxley equated humanity's situation with that of frogs, whose visual system only allows them to "see" movement. Whatever is stationary ceases to "exist for the frog".[239] Psychologist Robert Ornstein points out that nature is a cold, quiet and colorless affair outside us. The temperature, colors, and sounds we experience are dimensions of the human experience and not of the world itself, Ornstein reminds us.[240]

Neuroscientist Karl Pribram and quantum physicist David Bohm, who was mentioned earlier, have proposed a model to help explain human consciousness. Their model provides insight as to why humans have such problems grasping the truth of their situation with their lenses and brains. Bohm and Pribram's writings intuit some key Sufi principles. For this reason, I want to explore them in more detail.

Their model involves holography, the specialized photography made possible by laser technology. A holograph film is produced when laser light is bounced off some object of interest, creating interference wave patterns. This process produces an interesting result. To the naked eye, a holographically exposed film captures no visible "image" as we know it. However, a laser light used to project the exposed film (much as a slide projector does) "reproduces" the object in a dramatic three-dimensional effect. What is captured holographically on the film totally challenges our very notion of what constitutes reality.

Film exposed to ordinary scattered light produces an instantly recognizable "object", a miniature (albeit a "negative") of what we see with our own eyes. In a holographic film, "objects" appear literally nowhere, yet are everywhere in the film. Such film can be cut out into many pieces, yet the entire "object" of interest remains in every piece. A holograph presents a different reality from that provided by a lens-defined or "objective" model of the world ("objective", as in the lens of a microscope, telescope or human eye).

Pribram is interested in the hologram as a model, or metaphor, to help explain certain brain functions, including such mysteries as memory loss. Our memory, for instance, seems to be distributed throughout the brain and located nowhere specifically. Other brain functions he sets out to explain include the maintenance of "constancy", or recognizing an object, regardless of its distance or orientation with respect to the viewer, and the transfer of skills from one limb of our body to another.

Bohm uses the hologram as a model to illustrate the existence of an "implicate reality" lying beyond the limits of our "explicate" senses. He offers the difference between the common photographic "negative" and the hologram as an analogy, respectively, of his "explicate" and "implicate" orders of reality.[241] He describes a new concept of "reality" for the theoretical physicist and the sensory scientist to consider. As indicated earlier, he makes it clear that we must cease to consider the particles, which physics had previously considered the basic constituents of matter, to be independent and separate.

The term "electron" should be viewed as no more than a name, a label that we use to call attention to a certain demonstrated phenomenon. It is an aspect that can be accurately discussed only in terms of an individual, material object moving independently in a specific location.

Thus, we come to a new general physical description in which "everything implicates everything" in an order of undivided wholeness. "All implicates all", even to the extent that we ourselves are implicated together with "all that we see and think about". So, we are present everywhere and at all times, though only implicately (that is implicitly). The same is true of every "object".[242]

Pribram suggests that scientific sense can now be made out of mystical experiences which people have been describing for millennia. Although what he states is not part of his own experience, he cannot help but wonder if somehow the mystics have not discovered a mechanism which permits them to tap into the order of reality that is behind the world of appearances, to tap into the implicate order. He believes that to do so would "be a matter of abrogating our retrieval systems so that we can experience the brain's minicodes".[243] We would ignore our senses or "lenses" and experience only the frequency domain.

The purpose of science is to make sense of the world, and mystical experience makes sense when one can provide the mathematical transform that one takes back and forth between the ordinary-imaged domain and the frequency domain.[244] Pribram is in agreement with the most basic teachings of the Sufis when he suggests that the mystics may have discovered a way to cognize Bohm's implicate order by learning ways to abrogate, or get around, our brain's retrieval systems and micro-electric codes.

In the best scientific tradition of open skepticism, Pribram admits no personal knowledge replicating such experiences for himself; instead he refers interested parties to the writings of the great mystics of history. Their writings suggest to him that some have discovered techniques to getting around or beyond the "explicate order", to behold the true nature of our reality as human beings.[245] It is extremely important that, for the first time in three centuries, science is exploring that the ground of all is enfolded in our consciousness. Pribram sees the very nature of the universe, of matter, of life and of consciousness as projections of a common ground.[246]

Hazrat Shah Maghsoud Sadegh Angha, the great Sufi of our time, tells us that true consciousness cannot be attained through the sensory modalities, which are the source of what we think as knowledge. He further tells us that there is more to human beings than their material dimension. Human consciousness of reality lies not in the brain's bio-computer but in electromagnetic fields and centers of our being and in our receptive capacities. The electromagnetic elements and connections are those aspects of being traditionally perceived as spiritual. The enlightened have always shared with the people of their time the ways and means of how they attained their wisdom and knowledge. But to receive unlimited truth, commonly used tools are insufficient due to their limitations.

Professor Sadegh Angha, in *The Mystery of Humanity*, tells us how to reach the highest spiritual level, which is beyond all the levels described and is the level of true consciousness. He states that only the concentration of energies on the "I" provides the harmony necessary for the unfolding and development of our innate potentials and discovering of our reality.[247]

The Concentration of Energies and the Discovery of "I"

The concentration of energies and the establishment of harmony are essential to discover and experience the eternal and heavenly dimensions of human beings that are otherwise inaccessible to the limited thoughts and emotions. The senses, with all their limitations, cannot guide us toward the path of self-discovery. The important point to recognize here is that, to discover the truth, one must be in harmony and have the capacity to accept. If this principle does not exist, any encounter will only be superficial.

To know reality, one must be in harmony with it; the discovery of the spiritual dimension depends on the receptivity of the seeker. Being receptive means having one's receptors activated and in harmony. For example, after a child is born, the more the mother caresses and cuddles the infant, the more his or her receptors are activated. This process enhances the child's receptivity on a physical and emotional level. Developmental research has established the critical importance of close tactile stimulation with human infants. As reported in most introductory developmental psychology texts, to deprive a child of it can mean severe physical and mental dysfunction, even death.

Just as it is necessary for our receptors to be developed on a physical level, it is equally important that we develop the receptors that involve our spiritual evolution, so that our capacity for the reception of spiritual matters can be attained. Sufism says that before we humans can truly communicate, lead, motivate, find peace, understand nature, promote human rights, or partake in any other endeavor, we must come to discover a hidden dimension within ourselves. This faculty, this receptor, enables us to cognize accurately our true situation, as Pribram speculated when he wrote about abrogating our retrieval system.

On any level of human interaction, harmony is necessary to establish communication; it takes harmony between the listener and speaker so that communication may take place. The fewer mental distractions the listener has, the more focused he or she is, the more he or she is capable of understanding what the speaker is saying. The same is required to discover the spiritual depth and subtleties of the words of God which are received through revelation. The human system has a built-in mechanism capable of receiving revelation. According to the teachings of the Oveyssi School of Sufism, the human body is equipped with 13 electromagnetic centers, whose function is vital to the well-being of individuals, as well as their metaphysical and spiritual life.

The most important of these centers resides in the heart. The cardiovascular system is the first system to function in the embryo. The earliest sign of the heart is the appearance of paired tissue during the third week of gestation. These cords then become tubes, which fuse to form a single chamber. With further development, because the ventricle grows faster than other regions, the cardiac tube bends itself, forming a U-shaped loop.

Contractions of the heart in the sinus venosus begin by the 21st/22nd day after conception. The site of our primordial biological pacemaker (that which controls the electrical activity of the heart) is in this primitive atrium. The Sino-atrial node develops during the fifth week of gestation. It is originally located in the right wall of the atrium, but, with further development of the heart, it becomes incorporated into the Crista Terminalis, which is the remnant of the sinus venosus, the site of the "primordial pacemaker".

According to the teachings of M.T.O. Shahmaghsoudi School of Sufism, this Crista Terminalis is the most important energy source of the body. My father, Molana Shah Maghsoud Sadegh Angha, who is the forty-first Master of the School, has referred to it as the "I", the "source of life in the heart".[248] This source is the gateway to the human being's spiritual realm, as it is the doorway to the heavenly kingdom of God. The energy created by this "primordial pacemaker" is closely tied in with the bioelectric mechanisms of the heart, as mediated by the cardiac plexuses (conglomerates of nerve fibers). The heart is innervated by those neurons in our autonomic nervous system that excites us (the sympathetic nerves) and calms us (the parasympathetic nerves). Our heart's excitation arises from the main trunk of neck and upper thoracic neurons of the right atrium of our heart.

Our 10th pair of cranial nerves, the vagus nerve, mediates the autonomic nervous system's role in exciting and calming our heart. This nerve consists of motor (efferent) neurons that innervate the muscles of the heart, through the nodes described earlier and the complex of neurons around the coronary arteries. The vagus nerve also includes sensory (afferent) neurons that relay messages back to the brain and take part in our cardiovascular reflexes. These afferent fibers, running with the sympathetic nerves, carry nervous impulses from the heart back to the central nervous system. These pathways are directed both, to the brain stem and cerebral cortex. We know, for example, that in cases where the blood supply to the myocardium (the muscular substance of the heart) becomes compromised, pain impulses reach consciously via this pathway.

As previously indicated, the importance of the heart is repeated throughout the Holy Qur'an and the Holy Bible. For example, prayer in Islam begins with the Sura al-Fatiha (1:1-7): "In the Name of God, the Compassionate, the Merciful - O God lead us to the Straight Path [...]." It is by straightening the connection between the heart and the brain that the brain is illuminated. In Western medicine, it is believed that the brain is the control center of the whole body. However, the heart is the ultimate center that commands the brain, which in turn commands the body. In other words, in Western tradition the primary relationship is:

Figure 13: The Relationship in Western Tradition

Whereas the ultimate relationship should be:

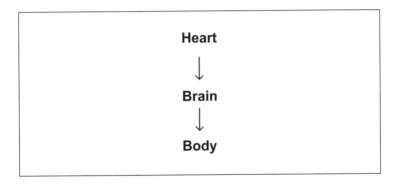

Figure 14: The Ultimate Relationship

In this light, the words of prayer take on a new meaning: the path between the heart and the brain becomes "straightened" or reversed.

In 1968, my father, in his book, *Message from the Soul*, wrote the following:

There are one hundred and one channels, starting from the source of life in the heart through which seventy one thousand lines irrigate the ten billion brain cells, so that the creation of God in this diffusion and gathering is brought to perfection. The source of life resides on the border between the heavens and the earth, and serves the will of God. At the point where the consciousness of life and the sleep of death confront each other, the first longs for eternity and the latter is attracted towards transience.

Search for truth in your heavenly double, at a third point in the heart, the point of union of the two worlds, one delicate and one harsh, between sleep and wakefulness. The source of life in the heart is the light of knowledge and certainty, and the very knowledge itself. And because it is all knowing, it is the source of all appearances and possibilities. It is the essence and the body of all things. Everything is brought to perfection by it.[249]

The point of union of the two worlds, the "Primordial Knot", is "dormant" for lack of a better term. Through meditation and prayer, it is "awakened" and the pathway between the heart and brain thus becomes "illuminated". A reversal occurs in the relationship between the two entities, in such a way that the "polarity" of the heart gains its due sovereignty over the realm of the previously mentioned opening verse of the Holy Qur'an.

The electrical properties of the heart have been used in Western medicine through the technology of the electrocardiograph, the EKG. The magnetic properties of the body, in general, and the heart, in particular, even though measurable, have been ignored by medical science because of a lack of understanding of their importance. And, unfortunately, because the electromagnetic centers of the body are not externally visible, their existence, function, and properties remain a mystery.

Revelation, like many other aspects of religion, has remained in obscurity and has usually been considered to be beyond the reach of human beings. As mentioned before, the human system has a built-in mechanism to receive revelation. It requires readiness and harmony on the part of the recipient. The field of electromagnetic centers and its relationship with the spiritual training received by the student of Sufism is extensive. Each of the 13 main centers has a specific function and is connected to special electromagnetic and universal energy sources. Discovery and development of this built-in mechanism transforms the individual and as a result, the organization's paradigm.

This is the true essence of education and development as the teaching of Sufism introduces them. In any discipline one must study and experiment under the instruction and guidance of a knowledgeable teacher to master one's subject. Likewise, it requires the presence of a spiritual master to discover the truth of the human being, and the road map to the eternal dimension. The Arif (Sufi) is one who has attained knowledge of reality, and can guide the seekers to overcome the obstacles of their journey toward self-knowledge.

5.4. The Teacher

Almost two and a half thousand years ago, Plato, in his famous Allegory of the Cave, described the perplexity of humanity's situation and state of "unfinished education".

He said:

"Shackled head and foot from birth to the cold wall of your cave, you sit mesmerized by the shadows cast by a bonfire out of your direct sight. In your ignorance, you mistake the shadows of real people and objects parading unseen behind you, for reality itself. Only after someone comes to deliver you miraculously from your chain, are you able to turn around, in pain and protestation, to behold your sad, deluded situation. Only then do you begin to see accurately the reality of events taking place in the cave. With further guidance, you ascend outside to behold the green grass, blue sky, fresh air and finally, the brilliant sun itself. Completing your education thus requires a teacher."[250]

Plato discovered from his own experiences that he was a prisoner of his senses. This ancient allegory, often treated as some abstract philosophical koan, suddenly becomes enormously relevant when one understands that one lives out one's life in just such a cave - the one atop the torso: the brain. This three-plus pound mass of protoplasm is the source and repository of all one's sensory perceptions, memories, emotions, learning - in short, all of human "psychology" ultimately resides somewhere in the brain's bio-chemical, electrical mini codes. And however differently one may sense reality, one will live one's entire life in a world of cortical shadows, out of which one constructs a limited and totally distorted reality of what "is". In the most literal sense, one is a cave dweller.

Modern scientific research, across many disciplines, has validated Plato's metaphor. In his book on human memory, science writer Philip Hilts made several observations about humanity's cave and the misapprehensions and misperceptions it creates. He presented several key principles in Sufism in a way seldom found in scientific writing. He stated that in everyday life we act as if we have a clear and complete depiction of the world outside us. Based on our limited sensory experiences, we imagine wholeness, and think we sense our entire world.[251]

There is an enormous disparity between this ordinary experience and what we know must exist. Our physical senses are only capable of distinguishing a minute portion of the electromagnetic spectrum, for example. Despite the new paradigms for science being postulated early in this century, we are just now beginning to understand them, and neither philosophy nor the social sciences have explored the possible consequences. Hilts postulates that, since it usually takes decades, perhaps centuries, for a radically different vision to be accepted and established, so it must be for this new understanding we are approaching.[252]

Scientists in other disciplines have also concluded that humanity's knowledge of reality remains shrouded and incomplete. Quantum physics, for instance, stated that humanity does not know reality. In fact, it said, we cannot even imagine it. Einstein's colleague, Sir Arthur Eddington, evoking Plato's imagery, once described humanity's situation as "watching a shadow graph performance of familiar life".[253]

As previously noted, both modern physics and biology state that humanity remains shrouded from the true reality of existence, believing only that it is what we see, hear, touch, taste and smell that exists. Things indeed are not as they seem! We must learn a radically new way of seeing, for humanity's education is incomplete.

The Holy Prophet Jesus (peace be upon him), who often commanded that "let he who has ears hear, and he who has eyes see", also said, "I shall give you what no eyes have seen and what no ear has heard and what no hand has touched and what has never occurred to the human mind".[254]

Vision is independent of muscles, eyelashes, nerves, and lenses. That is to say, vision is not bound by the physiological mechanisms of sight and hence does not limit itself to the eyes. Vision is infinite and absolute, although its manifestation is through the visual mechanisms named above. Vision is innately present in the human being, but since it is usually directed to the surface of things, its reality is hidden.

Hazrat Ali (peace be upon him), the revered Lord of the Sufis has said, "faith is manifested in the heart as a ray of light, and as faith increases, the light spreads".[255] Faith must be based on certainty, which comes from direct cognition or knowing. According to the teachings of the Oveyssi School of Sufism, the human body is equipped with a built-in mechanism that facilitates the ascension of the human being to the most elevated state. The prophets, saints, and the enlightened are examples of this ascendance. Every human being should become in harmony and on the same frequency so that one can discover the reality of "seeing" and "hearing". For this to take place, it is necessary that one be on the journey of ascent of the self.

Whatever existence has, human beings also have. All that exists is imbued with existence; nothing is apart from existence. To attain the state of "hearing" and "seeing", we must be elevated from the lowest state of our existence, which is our physical level to our most elevated state.

Sufism completes humanity's education. It answers ultimate questions about who we are, where we come from, and where we are going. It unchains the human being from the cave and allows one to cognize the reality underlying all of existence and to learn how to use wisely the riches bestowed by existence. A Sufi analogy says the banquet is already before humanity, but we simply do not experience it because we are looking the wrong way.

Molana Hazrat Shah Maghsoud states that "on the Journey, the Seeker needs a Teacher into whose care he is given, so that by the Teacher's guidance he may overcome the obstacles of the Journey. Knowledge without a teacher will not be profitable; and love without a Lover is without light, and devotion without the Beloved has no goal, purpose, or reality".[256] Safieddin Ardebili, the renowned 8th century Sufi, said, "the one who goes on this Journey on his own will drown in the mirage of the self. The body is nourished from the elements and the soul is nourished in hearing the words and heeding the guidance of the enlightened ones".[257] Rumi, the 13th century Sufi, stated, "whoever travels without a guide needs two hundred years for two days' journey".[258]

The Teacher, called the Arif, is the patient guide to spiritual ascension. The teacher is called "The Light of the Path", for he illuminates the darkness to help seekers to find their way. The presence of the Arif differentiates and characterizes Sufism, for the Teacher personifies what the Seeker wishes to attain. The word *Irfan* (Sufism) generally means cognition, and for the Arif it is the way to cognize the attributes and essence of Existence through the discovery of the eternal dimension and the secrets of man's heart through vision and revelation. The word cognition has also been used by philosophers. However, there is a great difference between the method of the Arif and that of the philosopher regarding the attainment of true cognition. The Arif cognizes the truth through certainty, heart-visions, and stability in the reality of identity of his true personality. But, for the philosopher, the method of cognition is based on reasoning, analogy, and logic, deduced from the mental faculties, from sensory inputs, and from observation of natural phenomena.

The Arif teaches that cognition can be obtained through self-discipline, purification, concentration, and meditation, as well as through prayer. The inner journey transforms human beings and deepens their level of awareness, until one moves from egocentric consciousness to awareness of the soul and spirit, and to oneness with reality. Sufi Meditation, called Tamarkoz, which differs markedly from what Westerners call Meditation, creates a state of equilibrium, balance and harmony. These powerful and precise methods of inward cognition and self-discovery align, balance, and activate the energy fields of the body, so the Seeker becomes receptive and in harmony to attain unity with the spirit. True meditation connects us with the fundamental unity of everything in the universe.

In any scientific experiment, three elements must exist: a laboratory, the subject of the experiment, and the scientist. In this context, the laboratory, the subject, and the scientist are one: the person who wants "to know", and is being taught by the Teacher how to conduct the experiment so that the anticipated results may be obtained. Through this method, the seeker's inherent abilities are developed and trained so that one may be united with one's eternal dimension and discover a vast sphere of awareness, knowledge, balance, harmony and love. When the Seeker experiences the reality of the Self, when he or she discovers the "I", the truth brings certainty as well as peace and tranquility to one's life. Certainty is the key word in the Arif's teachings; knowledge leads to certainty. It is important that we remember that freedom is not something that can be given to us, but rather it is a state we must create for ourselves no matter where or who we are. Freedom exists where knowledge exists.

Levy and Merry identify *Consciousness Raising* as a method of changing an individual's paradigms, which leads to corresponding changes in attitudes and behaviors. They argue that techniques and practical interventions, such as meditation and creativity exercises, transform the individual and subsequently the organization. They regret that so far there have been no systematic attempts to integrate concepts from Eastern and Asian philosophy into this strategy, and suggest further exploration and use of Eastern concepts of the individual, in organizational development and transformation strategies.[259]

The practice of Sufi concentration and meditation provides a remedy for the shortcomings of current organizational and personal transformation theories. It enables individuals to get in touch with their true consciousness. It goes beyond the domain of cognitive change, since it focuses on the unification of mind and heart, and opens the door to the unlimited dimension of human beings. The essence of true education and development leads individuals to a revolutionary paradigm change and fundamental personal and consequently, organizational wide transformation.

6. Conclusion

The late 20th century has witnessed the global reorganization of forces. The end of the Cold War resulted in the disintegration of the Soviet Empire and the emergence of new nation states. The new world order called for a fundamental rethinking of the relation between society, institutions, and the individual. New forces such as globalization, increased international competition, and cultural diversity initiated numerous changes in the way political and business leaders perform their roles. Within organizations, there has been a diminution of the vertical and horizontal walls that rigidly divided employees between departments. Organizational theory has developed new concepts such as flattening of organization, participatory management, total quality, shared vision, self-managed teams, and world-class manufacturing. Moreover, there has been increased emphasis on cooperation and collaboration, both at domestic and global levels. Many political divisions disappeared when Communist-dominated Eastern Europe fragmented into a multiplicity of nation states guided by principles of representative democracy.

The 21st century will see further efforts to promote unity and to establish democratic regimes around the globe. There will also be improvements in organizational management. Organizations can enjoy a high rate of productivity only if they have a committed and motivated workforce. The limitations of quality-focused approaches have become evident, and participatory management has become the proposed solution to many new/old problems. In management we have witnessed that the role of the individual, either as an employee or as a manager, has been the focus of many models and theories. In particular, there will be adjustments at the micro level, the individual level. The boundaries imposed on human beings by society should dissolve, so their inherent capabilities, potentials, and true value will blossom. This millennium will be the era of self-knowledge.

It is apparent that the current methods of management lack the required comprehensiveness and vastness required for the vitality and success of the organization. In the review of management history, we have witnessed major shifts in the dominating paradigms of each era and the evolution of management to this date.

In summary, we have reviewed how, during the era of Classical Management, the Classical Scientific School presented the individual as an "organizational man", one who through proper use of tools, motions, and time could be as efficient and productive as a machine, and monetary rewards would suffice to motivate him. Scientific Management improved productivity, but failed to recognize the potential of a human being, and degraded his/her value to the level of a machine or an efficient robot.

In the Classical Administrative School, the individual is considered to be a "social man". This school emphasizes the importance of the organizational environment, and how, through cooperation and improved relations, an organization can reach its goals. This theory values the social context of work, but ignores the individuality of the worker and the capabilities of a human being.

The major discovery of the Behavioral Management Schools was the recognition of workers' needs and motives. It was realized that concern for the welfare and individuality of the workers leads them to a strong commitment to the organization, therefore resulting in increased productivity. Numerous motivational theories emerged during this era that focused on both extrinsic and intrinsic motives and rewards. However, identifying innumerable needs and satisfying changeable needs of diverse employees became an almost impossible task. This theory focused on the individual, but with a limited perspective. However, at least it pointed to the right direction.

During the time of Management Science Theory, the concern for people changed to the use of quantitative methods. Companies became preoccupied with scientific management models and techniques, overlooked environmental changes, and disregarded the importance of human creativity and insight. The high price of losing many markets to foreign companies led management to the era of Systems Theory.

Systems Theory encourages managers to envision organizations as open systems. This approach facilitates participatory management at micro and macro levels of the organization. Managers need to assess the environments, modify their strategy, and adapt to changes. In this view a system is composed of many individual parts. Analyzing all parts and the relationships among them facilitates understanding the whole system. Even though this theory recognized the vitality of the organization as an open system, it totally ignored the vastness of the individual as an open system. The individual who constantly is exchanging information has an abundant source of creativity and capabilities.

The Systems approach led to Contingency Management Theory, which emphasizes that the best way to manage is determined by recognizing the contingencies that are present in a particular situation. Obviously, management has moved from the absolute to the relative. Contingency Theory is a radical departure from Classical Management Theory. The best way to manage has changed to the paradigm that there is no optimal way of management. In each situation, the key variables or contingencies need to be identified and certain managerial actions must take place. However, in an increasingly multinational environment and diverse workforce, application of the Contingency Management theory is a major challenge, particularly in a competitive market where the main objective is to increase productivity at the lowest possible cost.

This leads us to the period of Quality Control models and the re-enforcement of Participatory Management. Organization wide commitment to continuous process improvement, shared goals, employee empowerment, and customer satisfaction constitutes the core of the Quality Management model. However, the majority of corporate leaders are dissatisfied with the overall results of employing quality control methods such as TQM. The most critical factor for successful implementation of TQM is the commitment of the workforce. Achieving overall willingness and motivation through common goals in a society with a strong individualistic character is out of reach.

In regard to Management Information Systems (MIS), we noticed that the advancement of information technology and its application to management has given numerous advantage points to companies and organizations that have utilized it. However, the human factor has suffered. The new knowledge worker has to ratify the company's philosophy of rapid changes, continuous learning, and heavier responsibility. He/she has to face physical and emotional challenges, and still remain empowered, creative, dedicated, and committed. However, achieving the highest stage of moral evolution and having strong ethical principles do not bring about genuine change in the individual's paradigm. This brings us to the fundamental question: What is the force that empowers, and unleashes individuals'energy, commitment and enthusiasm? Is there a deeper insight, a higher dimension of the individual beyond the boundaries imposed by culture, society, race, gender, and ethnicity that can provide us with a formula to empower and manage?

In reviews of OD (Organizational Development) and OT (Organizational Transformation) and current change models, we noticed that these theories are built upon the conceptuality of an individual as a "social man". They lack the focus of the reality of the individual. At the macro level, the focus is to build coherence through corporate vision or shared goals. However, they do not penetrate deep into the individual consciousness to transform and change paradigms. At the micro level, the focus on the individual is limited to an outside-in approach. The stimuli, or the motivator, is always from the environment and not from within the individual. Therefore, change and personal transformation do not occur.

Most of the leadership theories have a contingency approach and still promote non-participatory methods in certain circumstances. In an ever-changing information era, the significance of participatory management at all levels is evident, and non-participatory styles are obsolete. At a micro level the focus of current leadership theories is on an outside-in approach, and again the comprehensiveness of an individual as a true open system is overlooked.

Principle-Centered Leadership promotes an inside-out approach. This theory emphasizes that the individuals can be empowered and motivated when they base their conduct on character ethic and fundamental principles. Unfortunately, in most situations we notice that individuals know the principles, but they lack the willingness, desire, or the strength to implement them. Furthermore, no attention is paid to the source of the principles.

By reviewing the major political, sociological and psychological theories, it becomes evident that theories of management are deeply rooted and closely interwoven with the dominant social sciences of their era. In turn, social science theories are based largely on theories of natural sciences in fields such as biology, chemistry, physics, etc. For example, we notice that our society and our organizations are still heavily influenced by "Newtonian images of the universe",[260] of three hundred years ago. Newton's model of the universe reflects a machine consisting of many parts. To understand the whole machine and its overall function, he suggests that one needs to separate the parts and analyze each piece in detail. Then, by putting it back together, the whole can be understood.

We used the Newtonian model to design and understand our organizations and our society. We divided the whole organization into departments and divisions, broke down the job into many measurable tasks, created many horizontal and vertical lines, and enclosed everything into boxes in organizational charts. We created limitations and boundaries in all directions. By becoming an expert reductionist, we lost the whole picture.

In Newtonian theory, two essential elements/factors are overlooked. First, the "knowledge" of the creator of the machine, and second the relationship between the parts and the overall synergy. If we omit the knowledge of the creator from the machine, what is left is a pile of metal, glass, battery, leather, plastics, etc. The knowledge of the creator is bestowed in what is created. In other words, what is created manifests the creator and the creator's knowledge. Through reduction, by analyzing each part in separation, and even by understanding the relationships between the parts in limitations, we cannot understand the whole. We do not discover the knowledge which exists and brings the machine as one whole unit into life.

This applies to human beings as well. A human being is created, he/she exists, and the knowledge of creation or existence is bestowed in him/her. He/she manifests the knowledge. He/she has it all; he/she is the true unit, which, in balance and harmony with existence, can reveal the knowledge of the creator, the knowledge of existence.

By focusing on the Newtonian model of the world, which is characterized by materialism and reductionism, we have deprived ourselves of recognizing the human being and his or her potential. We have failed to understand an individual as an open system who interacts with the whole environment and universe at large. "The Newtonian model of the world focuses on things rather than relationships."[261] and even when we bring our attention to the concept of "relationships" our focus is on the surface. We analyze phenomenon such as "team work" only on the surface. We do not penetrate and seek a deeper meaning. We do not look for a true source of coherence and cooperation. This is as true of political systems as it is of individuals and organizations.

A society or an organization built on a limited perception of the world does not search for solutions at a deeper level, based on the true, natural laws of existence. We do not look for a true source of coherence, or search for seemingly invisible relations and connections that influence our understanding of the whole. We do not seek a broader vision. Our limited comprehension of the laws of nature governing our society and our organizations does not reflect the advancements in science of our time. The science of the 20th century comes from the disciplines of physics, biology, chemistry, and from theories of evolution and chaos that span several disciplines.

Now that we are at the beginning of the new millennium, at least the science of our time should be applied. Early this century the world was introduced to the Quantum view of reality, the sub-atomic world of relations and connections. Quantum physics unfolded these invisible connections between parts that were previously thought to be separate. It makes us realize that space is not empty and everything in the universe is naturally connected, but it is invisible to the individual at his/her limited state of being. This perspective entirely changes our perception of the open system, both at micro and macro levels.

The current theories of leadership and motivation are people-oriented. However, they focus on limited aspects of the human being. Organizations are beginning to realize the wholeness of the individual. They recognize that the well-being of the individual can be achieved when different aspects of his/her life are in balance. Physical, emotional, mental, and spiritual balance is the key to the well-being of the individual as well as the whole organization. However, application of limited solutions and methods do not bring balance to life. The overall physics of our universe is about the eminence of relationships; the true laws of nature are limitless and apply to all levels. The human being is able to discover his/her inherent capabilities as a true open system only when in harmony with the laws of existence.

We hear that corporate and social culture, vision, and shared values have a strong impact on vitality and can bring about a successful change in an organization or a society. According to field theory, invisible forces structure space or behavior. In the application of field theory in management, it is assumed that the organizational vision is a field, a force of unseen connections that influence employees' behavior. However, this is a limited notion, for a force of unseen connections that influences behavior, the organization, and the society originates from deep within.

For any system to be formed first there must be attraction among the composing elements. It is the attractive field which is transformed into either energy or matter. The conversion of matter to energy and energy to matter is always through attraction. For the formation to actually take place, the attracting elements must converge into a state of harmony. If all employees are trained to develop their inner abilities, they will be in harmony and will be drawn by the attractive field. That is how coherence is achieved, commitment to common goals becomes realized, a shared vision is developed, and cooperation and collaboration is guaranteed.

In this era of self-knowledge, in a world where we talk about boundless organizations, self-managed teams and a self-renewing capacity of organizations, we need to realize that neither an organization nor a society is an entity independent of its people. An organization or a society is itself a conscious entity, possessing the properties of living systems. Individuals are the building blocks of organizations and societies and have such a capacity. The individual is capable of energizing, renewing, and creating continuously. This is possible only when the individual is in harmony and is connected to the essence of existence through the attractive field. The attractive field, the invisible force based on Sufi teachings, is the magnetic field; it is the "love" that connects all aspects of existence to each other. Hazrat Shah Maghsoud Sadegh Angha states: "Love is an all-pervading electromagnetic force, which unites and connects all aspects of existence, from the smallest particle to the whole infinite universe."[262]

At the beginning of the new millennium, we must realize that our current limited approaches are not effective. We cannot understand the whole by planning, analyzing, and dissecting the parts. We have limited ourselves to lines in all directions and have structured the parts in an attempt to mirror the whole. We need to realize that the era of linear planning is over. Existence tells us that in an infinite world the seemingly opposite reflections are simply two temporary manifestations of the one constant and stable reality. In our limited view of our environment, we perceive order vs. disorder; energy vs. matter; stability vs. change. However, the science of our time proves otherwise. The coherent evolution of one real system is manifested in seeming contradictions due to our limited view of the whole system.

The Hologram, Chaos, and Fractal theories demonstrate the unity of the whole universe. In the Hologram theory, "the part is in the whole and the whole is in the part"[263]; every part in its core manifests the whole. Chaos theory was revealed to us through modern computers. It reflects a system's movement from order to disorder. It demonstrates how a system moves from the state of order to oscillation to utter chaos, and when we expect everything to fall apart, magic happens. "The strange attractor comes into play; a strange attractor is a basin of attraction, and an area displayed in computer-generated phase space that the system is magnetically drawn into, pulling the system into a visible shape."[264] This point is reflected in many great writings by the Sufi of our time, Hazrat Shah Maghsoud Sadegh Angha. The so-called "strange attractor" is not at all strange to the knowledgeable. Each entity in this universe has its point of stability, which is the strongest magnetic center. Professor Sadegh Angha has called this luminous point, the "I", the source of life in the heart. The heart is referred to as the gateway to the unseen.

From the center of the heart, life unfolds itself in many different forms. The human body presents harmony and balance. In the human body each organ functions independently, and yet works in harmony with the rest of the system, for one purpose, the good of the whole, which ensures the survival of the parts. This law governs all entities in the universe. From the molecules, to the cells, to the organ, they work as a community and in harmony with each other, even though they live by the cellular law, which governs each individually. The reason for this vast cooperation is that each entity (from the small to the large) is submitted to its own inherent knowledge. The centrality of the heart is evident in the teachings of the Sufis. The center, the source of life, the "I" is located in the heart. It is the true fractal, the seed. The journey from the "I" to eternity begins here. All that is required is the seed and the gardener.

Already, a new revolutionary paradigm is emerging. It emphasizes the discovery of true human nature, the "I". It has become clear that addressing problems only at the macro level cannot yield long-term solutions. Transformation has to occur at the individual level. Personal transformation is the key to the success of political formations and organizations. Personal transformation resembles an internal revolution, because it signifies change that originates from the core of the individual's being. It cannot be initiated from the outside. Therefore, changes in social relations or improvements of the work process alone cannot lead to a fundamental change in the individual. Only when the revolution occurs in the core of the individuals' being, when they discover the "I", will cooperation, teamwork, cohesiveness, and creativity be inevitable outcomes.

Theory "I" provides a revolutionary and unlimited vision of leadership. It provides a blueprint for the ultimate personal transformation, which results in success and prosperity. Professor Sadegh Angha teaches that our desire to implement change, be it on the micro level or on the macro level, must begin with a transformation of the "i" into the "I". There is a fundamental difference between the "i", and the true "I". The "i" is subject to change and fluctuations. One cannot build upon an unstable foundation. Stable pillars must be erected upon stable centers.

Professor Sadegh Angha states: "What exists, in absolute rapture, glorifies the essence of being."[265] Human beings are no exception. When they are in harmony, oneness and unity will emerge. When all boundaries of separation and duality cease to exist, the image and its shadow will finally unite. Each entity in this universe has its source and center of stability. If one looks at the evolutionary stages of growth of the fetus, one realizes that in the beginning two energies named sperm and ovum contact each other. At the point of contact, conception occurs. Scientists state that a cell appears when physical, chemical, gravitational, and universal forces act in harmony. Being thus manifests itself in physical form, and leads to cellular division. The first heartbeat announces the beginning of a new life. The fetus spends nine months in the womb. At first, it is a collection of cells, a combination of the basic elements of oxygen, hydrogen, carbon, water, energies, and genetic information. Gradually, all embedded capabilities and potentials develop. The process of development is predetermined, orderly, and systematic. When this process is complete, the baby is born with full capabilities and potentials. Based on the unlimited and absolute laws of existence, the newborn person should continue to develop both physical and spiritual dimensions simultaneously. However, due to subsequent misteaching, and insufficient educational systems, only the physical aspects develop.

A person learns how to eat, walk, think, laugh, and cry. Unfortunately, for the majority of people, the developmental process comes to an end at this point. The unfolding of their potentials remains limited to their physical or material dimensions. The spiritual aspect, the "being" remains underdeveloped. Their true essence becomes buried under multiple layers of misteachings and limitations imposed by social norms and habits. When they encounter the concept of spirituality, they tend to deny the existence of such a dimension, because it does not have any relation to their material dimension. The artificial distance between the "i" and the "I", between the physical and the spiritual domains, remains intact. As a result, human beings lose touch with reality in its unified form due to boundaries imposed on body and mind.

To re-establish this lost harmony, to get back in touch with true reality, human beings have only one choice: They must return to their original source of life, to the "I", the point where "being" manifests itself in the form of matter. The concentration of dispersed energies and potencies in the center of the heart provides harmony and equilibrium. This way, we can access our lost spiritual dimension, and rediscover our source of tranquility. Discovery of the "I", the stable center, is the first step in the journey toward self-knowledge. This journey toward the realm of truth begins at the infinite center of the "I" and ends with absolute existence.

The human being is the building block of any social institution. If each individual rests in balance and utilizes his or her inherent capability, the same manifestation can be seen at every level of human organization. The discovery of the "I" results in the emergence of its principles. The principles of Theory "I" which are the fundamental principles of self-knowledge and were described in detail include:

- Principle of Prevalent, Informed Center

- Principle of Equilibrium and Balance

- Principle of Cooperation and Collaboration

- Principle of Comprehensiveness

- Principle of Harmony

- Principle of Guidance

- Principle of Love and Attraction

In an organization, the fundamental principles of Theory "I" manifest as follows:

Prevalent, Informed Center*...............................Creativity & Vision	
Equilibrium & Balance*..Stability	
Cooperation & Collaboration*.....................Teamwork & Coherence	
Comprehensiveness*..Synergy	
Harmony*...Compatibility	
Guidance*..Innate Knowledge	
*These principles manifest (become a reality) only in the presence of the ultimate principle: **Love & Attraction**	

Figure 15: Manifestations of Principles

Sufism teaches that for any system to be formed, first there must be attraction among the composing elements. This attractive field is the true source of coherence that brings all the elements composing that system together.

To illustrate this concept, let us consider a magnet and how it works. If we place a magnet on a surface and throw pieces of scrap metal around it, we notice that the scraps of metal become magnetized in the magnetic field of the iron and therefore are attracted to the source. They are submitted to the governing law of attraction. If we place pieces of rusted iron in the same magnetic field, no attraction takes place because there is no harmony. Connection occurs when the pieces or the scraps of iron are pure. Only when purified are they in harmony with their own essence and therefore in harmony with the source of attraction. As a result they are naturally attracted to the source. Attraction is possible only by submission to the essence and the governing laws, and submission is attained through purification.

This attractive field energizes and is the true source of action and motivation. The attractive field connects everything in the entirety of existence, from micro to macro and leaves no gap, no separation. Accessing the attractive field results in harmony, unity and true collaboration. Such an access is possible only through cognition of "I" and its principles.

Theory "I" is rooted in Sufism, and Sufism is generally accepted to be the mystical dimension of Islam. Although the origin of Sufism has been variously explained and interpreted, I would like to present the way I have experienced it. Sufism is the reality of religion. By this I mean experiencing God in one's inner self, submitting to Him, and loving Him with one's mind, heart and soul, until no other but the Beloved remains. This is the reality of religion, as I know it.

The word that captures the essence of Sufism is *Irfan*, derived from the word *ma'rifa* which means "knowing". In this context, it means knowing God and being replete with divine knowledge or mysteries. It is the way of the prophets. This is why I have defined Sufism as the reality of religion.

The urge to know is inherent in each human being. The quest for the meaning of life, for self-knowledge, for eternity, is timeless. It is not unique to any particular race, creed, or culture, nor bound to any particular place. It is universal. As it is written in the Holy Qur'an (21:7): "Before you, also, the apostles We sent were but men, to whom We granted inspiration [...]."

Those for whom the quest for the ultimate Reality is the most important goal in life, and who do not give up their search until they discover the answer, are generally regarded as "mystics". Mysticism is associated with mystery and the unknown. Often, it is associated with secret rites and special ceremonies for the initiated. Mysticism is the belief that union and absorption into God is possible through self-renunciation, contemplation and meditation. The mystical experience is considered to be one in which human reason has no part, being beyond human thinking or comprehension. In other words, it can only be known through personal experience. Therefore, the mind cannot grasp it and words cannot explain it. It is a mystery to those who have not had the experience. The mystical experience is usually associated with a sense of liberation, freedom, unity, contentment, abundance, compassion, knowledge, joy, and love.

The history of all religious traditions contains extensive accounts given by individuals who have undergone an experience that transcends the limitation of the senses. It is evident from these accounts that the intensity of the experience varies from one person to another. As these experiences come down to us they are frequently interpreted, formalized, ritualized and imitated. The true seeker, however, takes them as a signpost to persevere in his or her personal search for knowing the unknown. The seeker of God does not follow religion blindly, but searches for the truth within until the desired result is obtained.

The prophets, saints, and enlightened can be considered the true models of the genuine mystical experience. Their voices heralding their long-sought answers echo in the silent books. In finding the answer, their lives and visions were transformed. And their voices reach the hearts of genuine seekers who rise to search for the truth of their being.

Sufism teaches that all knowledge is humanity's legacy, but that one does not receive it until one truly seeks it. And, until it is fully experienced in one's own lifetime, the reality of the message of each prophet will never be known. Sufism is the essence of the prophets' teachings. It is the way of the prophets. It has existed since the beginning of human history, for its seed lies within every human heart. In each age, God has sent prophets to lead people to the knowledge of "Him" - Zoroaster, Moses, Buddha, Jesus, David, Mohammad (Peace be upon them) - to name a few. Each prophet has brought humanity a unique instruction to be learned and mastered in order to progress on the inward journey toward "God". The great ninth century Sufi, Bayazid Bastami, described the history of Sufism by stating: "Its seeds were set at the time of Adam, and they sprouted under Noah and flowered under Abraham. Grapes formed at the time of Moses, and they ripened at the time of Jesus. In the time of Mohammad, they were made into pure wine."[266]

Throughout time, people have attempted to express the ineffable quality of the mystical unity of all existence. This underlying unity has been the message of all religious traditions named above. However, external circumstances and ignorance have caused the alienation and misunderstanding that has existed and still exists among their followers. When religion becomes institutionalized, through time it becomes ossified and takes on the characteristics of the surroundings in which it grows. Slowly, its reason for having sprung to life is covered with superstition, dogma, ignorance and prejudice. The vibrancy of the message is lost in interpretation, rituals and blind faith. The personal discovery of the "mystery", which was the core of the prophets' beliefs and teachings, remains unknown to those who follow their words blindly.

Existing cultural, geographical, economic and political matters have colored people's perception of God. But, people's perceptions are not and cannot be the foundation of religion given by God. "Culture" means the behavior adopted by people and communities in direct response to their natural habitat and surroundings. Geographic location is the placement of the land with respect to the magnetic and gravitational changes on Earth. Politics is the presentation of some people's thoughts, needs, desires and self-interest, vis-à-vis those of others. Economics is the balance between our finite natural environment and the individual's infinite needs and desires.

Laws are meant to mediate between natural resources and the instruments used to maintain a balance of power among various political systems. They also protect the self-interest of individuals, groups, nation - states or regional alliances. The reality of religion transcends these concepts. The most profound mystical experience begins with knowing God and ends with the total absorption and annihilation of the self in God, where nothing but God exists. Each prophet voiced the experience of the discovered mystery - God. However, the experience was translated by people's imagination and existing religions, cultural and social factors, thereby giving different shapes, forms, attributes and characteristics to an experience that is unbounded and unquantifiable.

The point of divergence in all religious traditions takes place when the experience is formulated into words and images in the minds of those who have not had the experience themselves. The point of convergence is the experience of the one Reality. In the Holy Qur'an (21:92) it is written: "Verily, this Brotherhood of yours is a single Brotherhood, and I am your Lord and Cherisher: therefore worship Me." Only the Reality within us can guide us to the Reality; only when the transient becomes the Reality can one say: "I am the Reality". The expression of union or oneness express-ed in the proclamation of faith in Islam is: *La-ilahail'-Allah* - "There is no other than God." Physicist David Bohm's general law, described earlier, states that "everything implicates everything". There is no existence but existence. There is no reality but reality. This is the first law of Islam: *La-ilahail'Allah*. It is through submission that the state of oneness is attained. This means that the will of the individual is dissolved in the will of the Absolute, whereby the boundaries of individuation and limitation are demolished. The words of Amir-al Moemenin Ali, the guiding light for humanity, attest to this genuine and sacred goal: Islam is submission, and submission is stability and constancy in the true reality of Existence.

The constant determining factor that keeps all particles in balance on the plane of existence is the law of submission. Whenever we compare the structure of the solar system with the structure and organization of the atomic structure, we observe that within each element of the earth and other planets of the solar system, they all follow one all-pervasive law, the law of submission. They all are submitted to the innate knowledge and are governed by the laws of existence. So too is the human being who is able to cognize the "I", the source of knowledge. This is the state of total freedom and love which has been amplified in the writings of the Sufi Masters.

For 1,400 years, an unbroken succession of spiritual Masters have transmitted the tradition through Maktab Tarighat Oveyssi (M.T.O.) Shahmaghsoudi School of Islamic Sufism, leading seekers through the perils and pitfalls of the journey to self-knowledge. This knowledge has been passed directly from Master to Master over the centuries, so that those who seek to attain it will be guided toward such a goal. The M.T.O. Shahmaghsoudi School of Sufism dates back to the Holy Prophet of Islam, Prophet Mohammad, and then to Imam Ali (peace be upon them), the first Imam of the Shi'a. The founder of the School of Sufism is Oveys Gharani, who lived in Yemen at the time of the Holy Prophet. Without ever meeting the Prophet Mohammad, Hazrat Oveys received the teachings of Islam inwardly through his heart, and lived by the principles taught by him. At times the prophet would say of him: "I feel the breath of the Merciful, coming to me from Yemen". The Holy Prophet had his cloak sent to Hazrat Oveys, an event signifying his holy dignity. His way of cognition was confirmed as the Holy Prophet Mohammad said: "Follow the way of Oveys." And: "He is the pre-emptor of my genus." Hazrat Oveys' famous aphorism is: "Keep thy heart."

Since Hazrat Oveys' time, the cloak has symbolized the highest level of inspired divine knowledge and the light of guidance. It has been handed down through an unbroken succession of forty spiritual teachers, well known to historians and scholars, to Hazrat Molana Shah Maghsoud Sadegh Angha, and was bestowed upon me by him. My great-grandfather, grandfather and father had all been Masters of the Oveyssi School of Sufism, and all have always said that spiritual learning and development is a matter of personal effort and discovery. The teaching of Hazrat Imam Mohammad Bagher, the fifth Imam of the Shi'a, clearly illuminates the path of knowledge for the true seeker. He states: The teacher, the spiritual guide, is a pure essence which must be introduced (revealed) by God to the seeker's heart through his divine light.

The spiritual teacher, known as the Pir, meaning "the light of the path", guides the seeker through this process of discovery of "I". The Pir enables the seeker to liberate himself/herself from the imaginary boundaries and layers of ignorance and misteachings. The spiritual teacher provides the guidance of one who has been there, and knows the way to attaining the purification and the highest wisdom. The Pir teaches students how to purify and re-gain the lost harmony, and leads the seeker to his/her source of knowledge, to the "I". The guiding light of the teacher illuminates the seeker's path, and enables the seeker to overcome the obstacles. The seeker continues his/her journey of self-knowledge and discovers his/her true identity. Through cognition of "I" the seeker accesses the field of attraction and experiences cooperation, synergy, creativity, vision, teamwork, compatibility and leadership. Through this process of self-knowledge he/she becomes a leader, a leader who leads a life full of prosperity, peace, and true satisfaction ... a leader whose vision, creativity and wisdom are not limited by the imaginary boundaries and layers of misteachings ... a leader who is empowered by his/her own genuine source of energy and guidance ... a leader who can create and promote a nourishing environment of love, trust and collaboration. Leadership, therefore, is the creative capacity to evoke the most positive capabilities and potentialities within ourselves, and consequently, within others.

Hazrat Shah Maghsoud Sadegh Angha states: "When nature wanted to manifest itself in its most subtle of forms, it became an entity called the human being."[267] The goal of Theory "I" is to introduce human beings to their source of knowledge, tranquility and survival. It will enable them to discover their true reality and innate greatness. Human beings are the basic units of existence. Since existence is infinite, the true capabilities and potentials of each individual are also infinite. Human beings constantly seek tranquility through temporary joys and excitements, unstable relationships, and endless struggles to acquire more material possessions, or to achieve higher status in society. They incessantly try to be content, to be satisfied, and to be happy. "Whatever rank or position people may have, the goal of all of their efforts is to attain tranquility, whether this effort is expended in material, nonmaterial, or spiritual endeavors."[268]

Human beings constantly flow on the surface of their existence. Unable to penetrate to the depths of their being, they cannot experience tranquility. Hazrat Shah Maghsoud Sadegh Angha states: "Tranquility in its true meaning is defined as absolute harmony and unity. Survival then is a guaranteed outcome."[269] To achieve harmony it is necessary to remove artificial distances, gaps, and boundaries between the "i" and the true "I". Moreover, all limited perceptions and unreal labels must be removed in order for individuals to discover their true stable center, the "I".

Discovery of the "I", the source of life, is the beginning of the journey toward self-knowledge. It is here where materialist human nature yields to the spiritual dimension, which leads on a straight path from the stable center, the "I", toward absolute truth. In total harmony, one then explores and discovers many states of consciousness, until only one's essence remains. When they discover their stable center, human beings are released from the limitations of their materialist dimension, and the absolute laws of existence govern their lives.

A human being is like a complete book. To read our book we must learn its alphabet. The prophets have said that to read our book, we must return to our origin, to the source of being. Hazrat Mir Ghotbeddin Mohammad Angha has said:

If only the alphabet of the one spiritual book were revealed to man, and the secret of the book of the soul discovered, we would need none of the words sealed in silent books, and yet would know the story whole.[270]

The true meaning of education is learning the alphabet of the book of one's own being. This enables us to discover the hidden and unknown dimensions of our being, and our lives will be founded upon knowledge, and lead us to stability, tranquility, and peace.

We must not think that we need to undertake monumental and intricate projects to attain this goal. Instead of persistently trying to design and implement the illusory ideals of societies or organizations, thinkers and managers should put their efforts toward providing the means that will help individuals to discover their values. If all human beings are trained to develop all their inherent talents and abilities, they will be able to enjoy prosperity, creativity, happiness, and equality. Educational systems and training programs should be revised for individuals to be effectively educated, and to bring out their true capabilities and potentials. Educational systems should provide an environment conducive to developing each person's talents and abilities. Theory "I" introduces the concepts, and the educational methods for guiding each individual to his or her inherent values, as well as to true harmony and knowledge.

In contrast to the dominant misteachings, discovery of the true self is not attained through hardship. We hear from society that we have to bear hardship and eliminate joy, in order to gain wisdom. This is not possible. How can I grow wisdom from hardship? What I need to do is to purify, to unfold the mystery, to be a "human being". Sufism is not about "human doing". I do not have to go and do and create, but just to be, to be the real self. It is about discovering the reality of human being. It is about discovering the real being that you cannot see unless you remove the veil of ignorance through purification. When the individual begins to purify himself or herself, gradually the spark of light, the knowledge will guide throughout all aspects of life, from physical to spiritual.

Wisdom and knowledge cannot be imposed or given to anyone. It takes a sincere aspirant who makes every effort to discover the ultimate gift of existence: Self-knowledge. The seeker who undergoes the various stages of self-discipline and purification and for whom the veils of the unknowns have been lifted, with faith and knowledge, attests to the Oneness of God. He or she knows that there is neither duality nor separation between him or her and Existence, for whatever exists in submission forever glorifies the essence of Existence. The reality of submission is seen in the bloom of the rose, in the apple tree bearing healthy apples, in the brilliance of the moon. Each one manifests one law: submission to knowledge. It is knowledge that is capable of manifesting the rose, the tree, and all else in their completeness.

Sufism, in essence, is a method, a way, a discipline that teaches each person the science of exploring his/her being, discovering his/her hidden potentials, and the reality of his/her being in this unbounded and infinite tapestry called Existence. This process is not the result of the functioning of the mental faculties, i.e. induction, deduction, analysis, etc. It is the method and the way through which the Sufis attained the absolute state of cognition. The human being is naturally connected with the essence of Existence at the core of his/her being, but it is invisible to him/her. When the dynamic evolution and revolution take place at the core of the human being, all boundaries of separation cease to exist and the real relations become visible. It is through this connection that he/she becomes empowered, motivated, energetic, enthusiastic, dedicated, and truly alive.

When people are trained to discover this inner dimension of their being, then willingly they will leave behind their savage attributes which give rise to greed, envy, and prejudice. What is the result of such a discovery? If each person is trained to stand on his or her own strength, will they be needy? Will they not see their own uniqueness and the strength that this uniqueness brings? If each person is trained to develop his or her own talents and abilities, will there be any room for insecurity, jealousy, envy, or lack of trust?

Only a society whose individual members have recognized their true value and identity can reach a stage of health, balance, harmony, and collaboration. The leaders of such a society will adhere to noble and universal laws, consequently the principles of Theory "I" prevail, and each individual will develop a new vision of life beyond the confines of social rules and dominating paradigms.

Notes

[1] Talcott Parsons, *Theories of Society: Foundations of Modern Sociological Theory* (New York: Free Press of Glencoe, 1961), pp. 61-75.
[2] Robert A. Divine, T. H. Breen, George M. Fredrickson, R. Hal Williams, *America: Past and Present* (New York: Harper Collins, 1984), pp.788-790.
[3] Samuel Yellen, *American Labor Struggles* (New York: Arno and New York Times, 1969), pp. 298-301, p. 321.
[4] Leslie W. Rue, Lloyd L. Byars, *Management: Theory and Application*, 4th ed. (Homewood, IL: Irwin, 1986), p. 40.
[5] Ibid., p. 47.
[6] Richard L. Daft, *Management* (Orlando: Dryden Press, 1994), p. 63.
[7] W. Richard Plunkett, Raymond F. Attner, *Introduction to Management,* 5th ed. (Belmont, CA: Wadsworth Publishing, 1994), p. 37.
[8] Ibid., pp. 44-45.
[9] Harwood F. Merrill, *Classics in Management* (New York: American Management Association,1960), p. 29.
[10] Ibid., p. 14.
[11] Richard M. Hodgetts, *Management Fundamentals* (Hinsdale, IL: Dryden Press, 1981), p. 8.
[12] Merrill, *Classics in Management,* pp. 70-72.
[13] Ibid., p. 137.
[14] Plunkett, Attner, *Introduction to Management,* p. 38.
[15] Merrill, *Classics in Management,* p. 273.
[16] Cited in W. Jack Duncan, *Great Ideas in Management: Lessons From the Founders and Foundations of Managerial Practice*

(San Francisco: Jossey-Bass, 1989), p. 115.
17 Ibid., pp. 114-116.
18 Plunkett, Attner, *Introduction to Management,* p. 38.
19 Justin G. Longenecker, Charles D. Pringle, *Management*, 6th ed. (Columbus, OH: Charles E. Merrill Company, a Bell and Howell Company, 1984), p. 27.
20 Duncan, *Great Ideas in Management,* p. 179.
21 Daft, *Management,* p. 44.
22 Longenecker, Pringle, *Management,* p. 30.
23 Max Weber, *General Economic History* (New York: Collier, 1961), pp. 320-40.
24 Daft, *Management,* p. 45.
25 Duncan, *Great Ideas in Management*, p. 72.
26 Henri Fayol, *General and Industrial Management,* translated by J.A. Conbrough (Geneva: International Management Institute, 1929).
27 Rue, Byars, *Management: Theory and Application,* p. 39.
28 Adapted from Henri Fayol, *General Principles of Management* (Belmont, CA: Pitman Learning, 1949) in: Plunkett, Attner, *Introduction to Management,* p. 40.
29 Rue, Byars, *Management: Theory and Application,* p. 39.
30 Daft, *Management,* p. 40.
31 Plunkett, Attner, *Introduction to Management,* p. 42.
32 Longenecker, Pringle, *Management,* p. 33.
33 Merrill, *Classics in Management,* pp. 341-342.
34 Ibid., p. 350.
35 Longenecker, Pringle, *Management,* p. 35.
36 Duncan, *Great Ideas in Management,* p. 213.
37 Ibid., p. 213.
38 Daft, *Management,* p. 47.

[39] Longenecker, Pringle, *Management*, pp. 37-39.
[40] Plunkett, Attner, *Introduction to Management,* p. 42.
[41] Merrill, *Classics in Management*, p. 16.
[42] Duncan, *Great Ideas in Management*, p. 213.
[43] Reece McGee and others, eds., *Sociology: An Introduction.* (Hinsdale, IL: Dryden Press, 1977), pp. 12-15.
[44] Robert Owen, *A New View of Society,* First American Edition, from the Third London Edition. (New York, NY: L. Bliss & E. White Publishing, 1825), pp. 57-62.
[45] Merrill, *Classics in Management*, p. 20.
[46] Mary Parker Follett, *Business Management as a Profession.* (Chicago, IL: A.W. Shaw Company, 1927), pp. 73-87.
[47] Merrill, *Classics in Management*, p. 406.
[48] Ibid., p. 163.
[49] Robert N. Lussier, *Management Fundamentals* (Springfield, MA: Southwestern College Publishing, 1999), pp. 422-423.
[50] Duncan, *Great Ideas in Management*, pp. 164-165.
[51] Ibid., p. 165.
[52] Ibid., p. 167.
[53] Victor H. Vroom, *Work and Motivation* (New York: Weily, 1964), p. 232.
[54] Daft, *Management*, pp. 536-538.
[55] Douglas, McGregor, *The Human Side of Enterprise* (New York, NY: McGraw-Hill Company, Inc., 1960), pp. 37-42.
[56] Ibid., p. 45.
[57] Duncan, *Great Ideas in Management*, pp. 187-188.
[58] Ibid., p. 216.
[59] Hodgetts, *Management Fundamentals*, p. 17.
[60] Longenecker, Pringle, *Management*, p. 33.

61   Plunkett, Attner, *Introduction to Management*, p. 42.
62   Duncan, *Great Ideas in Management*, pp. 157-158.
63   Ibid., p. 179.
64   McGregor, *The Human Side of Enterprise*, pp. 33-70.
65   Daft, *Management*, p. 50.
66   Quoted in Duncan, *Great Ideas in Management*,
     p. 162.
67   Ibid., p. 163.
68   Plunkett, Attner, *Introduction to Management*, p. 411.
69   Ibid., p. 44.
70   Duncan, *Great Ideas in Management*, p. 72.
71   Ibid., pp. 72-73.
72   Ibid., p. 173.
73   Plunkett, Attner, *Introduction to Management*, p. 46.
74   Daft, *Management*, p. 54.
75   Plunkett, Attner, *Introduction to Management*, p. 46.
76   Ibid., pp. 44-46.
77   Longenecker, Pringle, *Management*, p. 189.
78   Ibid., p. 190.
79   Ibid., pp. 36-37.
80   Ibid., p. 37.
81   Plunkett, Attner, *Introduction to Management*, p. 48.
82   Mark R. Edwards, J. Ewen, *360° Feedback: The
     Powerful Model for Employee Assessment and
     Performance Improvement* (American Management
     Association,1996), pp. 4-8.
83   Longenecker, Pringle, *Management*, p. 41.
84   Plunkett, Attner, *Introduction to Management*, p. 49.
85   Philip Kotler, *Marketing Management: Analysis,
     Planning, Implementation, and Control* (Englewood
     Cliffs, NJ: Prentice Hall, 1997), pp. 20-24, p. 26.
86   Gerald H. Graham, *Management: The Individual, the
     Organization, the Process* (Belmont, CA: Wadsworth
     Publishing, 1975), p. 19.

87 Daft, *Management*, p. 57.
88 Longenecker, Pringle, *Management*, p. 42.
89 Ibid., p. 41.
90 Duncan, *Great Ideas in Management*, p. 238.
91 Daft, *Management*, pp. 503-512.
92 Plunkett, Attner, *Introduction to Management*, pp. 446-447.
93 Daft, *Management*, p. 508.
94 William G. Ouchi, *Theory Z: How American Busi- Can Meet Japanese Challenge* (Reading, MA: Addison-Wesley, 1981), p. 58.
95 Daft, *Management*, p. 59.
96 Longenecker, Pringle, *Management*, p. 43.
97 Ibid., p. 41.
98 Rue, Byars, *Management*, p. 51.
99 Daft, *Management*, p. 508.
100 Richard L. Williams, *Essentials of Total Quality Management* (New York, NY: American Management Association, 1994), p. 7.
101 Daft, *Management*, pp. 59-61, pp. 642-647.
102 Ibid., p. 755.
103 Japan Human Relation Association, *Teian Kaizen: Developing Systems for Continuous Improvement Through Employee Suggestions* (Productivity Press, 1992), p. 117.
104 Daft, *Management*, p. 647.
105 Williams, *Essentials of Total Quality Management*, p. 52.
106 James A. O'Brien, *Management Information Systems: A Managerial End User Perspective, 2nd ed.* (Home wood, IL: Irwin, 1993), p. 6.
107 Ibid, p. 37.
108 Steffano Korper, Juanita Ellis, *E-Commerce: Building the E-Empire*, 2nd ed. (San Francisco, CA:

Academic Press, 2001), p. 212.
[109] Amy Zuckerman, *Tech Trending: The Technology Survival Guide for Visionary Managers*, 1st ed. (United Kingdom: Capstone Publishing Limited, 2001), p. 319.
[110] Ibid, p. 8.
[111] Erik Brynjolfsson, Lorin Hitt, *The Customer Counts* (Information Week, Sept. 9, 1996), pp. 48-54.
[112] John Seely Brown, *Tools@work: Deciphering the Knowledge Management Hype* (Journal for Quality and Participation, special issue on Learning and Information Management. July/Aug. 1998, vol. 21, No. 4), pp. 58-60.
[113] Brian W. Arthur, *Increasing Returns and Path Dependence in the Economy* (Ann Arbor: University of Michigan Press, 1994).
[114] Karl Erik Sveiby, *The New Organizational Wealth: Managing and Measuring Knowledge-Based Assets,* 1st ed. (San Francisco: Berrett-Koehler Publishers), pp. 46-48.
[115] Sveiby, in: *Tools@work*, pp. 58-60.
[116] Paul Strassmann, *The Squandered Computer* (New Canaan, CT: Information Economic Press, 1997), pp. 108-113.
[117] O'Brien, *Management Information Systems*, p. 556.
[118] Ibid. O'Brien draws some of his examples from Gerald Baxter, Charles Rarick, *Ethical Issues in Information Systems* (Boston: Boyd & Fraser, 1991), p. 545.
[119] Ibid.
[120] Roger Nagel, Rick Dove, *21st Century Manufacturing Enterprise Strategy: An Industry Led View of Agile Manufacturing*, Vol. 1 (Bethlehem, Pennsylvania: Iacocca Institute, Lehigh University, 1991).

[121] William H. Davidow, Michael S. Malone, *The Virtual Corporation* (New York, NY: Edward Burlingame Books/Harper Business, 1992), pp. 184-216.

[122] Adapted from Jerry I. Porras, Robert C. Silver, *Organization Development and Transformation,* in: Wendell L. French, Cecil H. Bell, Robert Zawacki, *Organization Development and Transformation: Managing Effective Change* (Burr Ridge, IL: Irwin, 1994), p. 83.

[123] Ibid., p. 94.

[124] Ibid., p. 99.

[125] James M. Kouzes and Barry Z. Posner, *The Leadership Challenges* (San Francisco, California: Jossey-Bass Publishers, 1995), pp. 30-31.

[126] Idem, *The Seven Habits of Highly Effective People: Restoring the Character Ethic* (New York: Simon and Schuster, 1989), p. 18, p. 32.

[127] Ibid., pp. 33-34.

[128] Ibid., pp. 126-127.

[129] Albert Hourani, *A History of the Arab Peoples* (Cambridge, MA: Belknap Press of Harvard University Press, 1991), p. 145.

[130] Juan J. Linz, *An Authoritarian Regime: The Case of Spain,* in: Erik Allardt and Yrjo Littunen, eds., *Cleavages,* Ideologies and Party Systems (Helsinki: Westermarck Society, 1964), p. 255.

[131] Leonardo Morlino, *Authoritarianism,* in: Anton Bebler, Jim Seroka, eds., *Contemporary Political Systems: Classification and Typologies* (Boulder, CO, and London: Lynne Rienner Publishers, 1990), pp. 95-99.

[132] Billy Dudley, *An Introduction to Nigerian Government and Politics* (London: Macmillan, 1982), p. 70.

[133] Peter H. Koehn, *Public Policy and Administration in Africa: Lessons from Nigeria* (San Francisco:

Boulder, London: Westview, 1990), p. 76.
134 Ibid., p. 46.
135 Ibid., p. 47.
136 Ali D. Yahaya, *The Idea of Local Government in
     Nigeria: The Need for a Redefinition,* in: Abubakar
     Yaya Aliyu, ed., *The Role of Local Government in
     Social, Political and Economic Development in Nige-
     ria 1976-79* (Zaria: Department of Local Government
     Studies, Institute of Administration, A.B.U.).
137 Koehn, *Public Policy and Administration in Africa:
     Lessons from Nigeria,* p. 25.
138 Abdulaziz Al-Sweel, *Saudi Arabia: A Kingdom in
     Transition* (Beltsville, Maryland: Amana Public-
     tions,1993), p. 48.
139 Quoted in Ibid., pp. 50-51.
140 Ibid., pp. 58-61.
141 Mordechai Abir, *Saudi Arabia in the Oil Era: Regime
     and Elites; Conflict and Collaboration* (London and
     Sydney: Croom Helm, 1988), p. 216.
142 John S. Reshetar, Jr., *The Government of the Soviet
     Union,* in: Michael Curtis, ed. *Introduction to Com-
     parative Government,* 2nd ed. (New York: Harper Col-
     lins, 1990), p. 346.
143 Ibid., p. 340.
144 Ibid., p. 359.
145 Zbigniew Brzezinski, *Concluding Remarks,* in:
     Dilemmas of Change in Soviet Politics, ed., idem
     (New York: Columbia University Press, 1969), p. 152.
146 Red Flag, No. 3, 1972, in: FBIS (March 29, 1971),
     quoted in: James D. Seymour, *The Government of
     China,* in: Curtis, ed., *Introduction to Comparative
     Government,* p. 420.
147 Ibid., p. 422.

148 Nicholas Kristof, *Riddle of China: Repression and Prosperity can Coexist* (The New York Times, Sept. 7, 1993), p. A1.

149 Jie Chen, Peng Deng, *China Since the Cultural Revolution: From Totalitarianism to Authoritarianism* (Westport, CT, and London: Praeger, 1995), p. 8.

150 This is a simplified version of: Arend Lijphart, *Democratic Political Systems,* in: Bebler, Seroka, *Contemporary Political Systems,* pp. 71-90.

151 Ian Budge and David McKay, eds., *The Developing British Political System: The 1990s,* 3rd ed. (London and New York: Longman, 1993), p. 5.

152 Ibid., p. 210.

153 Dennis Kavanagh, *Changes in the Party System,* in: Jack Hayward, Philip Norton, eds., *The Political Science of British Politics* (Brighton: Wheatsheaf Books, 1986), p. 103.

154 Budge, McKay, eds., *The Developing British Political System: The 1990s,* p. 2.

155 Graham Wilson, *Changing Networks: The Bureaucratic Setting for Government in Political Science,* pp. 50-51.

156 Anthony King, *Cabinet Co-ordination or Prime Ministerial Dominance? A Conflict of Three Principles of Cabinet Government,* p. 52.

157 Melvyn Read, *The Place of Parliament,* p. 66.

158 Ivor Crewe, *Parties and Electors*, p. 111.

159 Ibid., p. 5.

160 Max J. Skidmore, Marshall Carter Wanke, *American Government: A Brief Introduction* (New York: St. Martin's Press, 1981), pp. 8-9.

161 Samuel P.Huntington, *American Politics: The Promise of Disharmony* (Cambridge, MA: Harvard University Press,1981), pp. 122-129.

[162] Lawrence C. Dodd, *The Rise of the Technocratic Congress: Congressional Reform in the 1970s,* in: Richard A. Harris, Sidney M. Milkis, eds., *Remaking American Politics* (Boulder, CO: Westview, 1989), pp. 89-90.

[163] R. Shep. Melnick, *The Courts, Congress, and Programmatic Rights,* in: Harris, Milkis, eds., *Remaking American Politics* (Boulder, CO: Westview, 1989), p. 208.

[164] Michael Parenti, *Democracy for the Few,* 5th ed. (New York: St. Martin's Press, 1988), p. 213.

[165] Alexis de Tocqueville, *Democracy in America* (New York: Knopf, 1835, Reprint 1951).

[166] Michel Crozier, *La société bloquée* (Paris: Seuil,1970).

[167] Mark Kesselman, *Over Institutionalization and Political Constraint: The Case of France,* in: *Comparative Politics,* Vol. 3 (City University of New York, 1970), pp. 21-44.

[168] Roy C. Macridis, *Modern Political Systems: Europe* (Englewood Cliffs, NJ: Prentice Hall, 1990), pp. 281-327.

[169] Ibid.

[170] David Arter, *The Nordic Parliaments: A Comparative Analysis* (New York: St. Martin's Press, 1989), pp. 415-416.

[171] Roland Huntford, *The New Totalitarians* (New York: Stein & Day, 1972), p. 10.

[172] Ibid., p. 348.

[173] Theodore McNelly, *The Government of Japan,* in: Curtis, ed., *Introduction to Comparative Government,* p. 279.

[174] Ibid., p. 307.

[175] Zhao Quansheng, *Japanese Policymaking: The Politics Behind Politics* (Westport, CT and London:

Praeger, 1993), p. 201.

176 Chalmers Johnston, *Political Institutions and Eco-nomicPerformance: The Government Business Relationship in Japan, South Korea, and Taiwan,* in: Tobert Scalapino, Seizaburo Sato, Jusuf Wanandi, eds., *Asian Economic Development - Present and Future* (Berkeley, CA: Institute of East Asian Studies, University of California, Berkeley 1985), p. 65.

177 Jon Woronoff, *Politics the Japanese Way* (London: MacMillan, 1988), p. 416.

178 Ibid., p. 419.

179 Ibid., p. 421.

180 Ibid., p. 424.

181 Madhu Limaya, *Will the Indian State Degenerate Into a Coercive One?* (Times of India, Oct. 12, 1989).

182 Thomas G.C. Raju, *Democracy, Security, and Development in India* (New York: St. Martin's Press, 1996), p. 153.

183 A.H. Somjee, *The Democratic Process in a Developing Society* (New York: St. Martin's Press, 1979), p. 153.

184 Lucile Duberman, Clayton A. Hartjen, *Sociology* (Glenview, IL: Scott Foresman, 1978), p. 4.

185 McGee, and others, eds., *Sociology: An Introduction,* p. 11.

186 Ibid., p. 12.

187 Ibid., p. 16.

188 Ibid., p. 20.

189 Ibid., p. 12.

190 J. Ross Eshleman, Barbara G. Cashion, and Lawrence A. Basirico, *Sociology: An Introduction,* 4th ed. (New York: Harper Collins, 1993), p. 36.

191 Ibid., pp. 36-37.

192 McGee and others, eds., *Sociology: An Introduction,* pp. 14-15.

[193] Eshleman, Cashion, Basirico, *Sociology: An Introduction,* p. 35.

[194] McGee and others, eds., *Sociology: An Introduction,*
p. 16.

[195] Richard T.Shafeer, *Sociology* (New York: McGraw-
Hill, 1989), p. 16.

[196] McGee and others, eds., *Sociology: An Introduction,*
pp. 18-19.

[197] Ibid., p. 21.

[198] Eshleman, Cashion, Basirico, *Sociology: An Introduction,* pp. 38-39.

[199] McGee and others, eds., *Sociology: An Introduction,*
p. 20.

[200] Beth B. Hess, Elizabeth W. Markson, Peter J. Stein,
Sociology, 4th ed. (New York: McMillan, 1993),
p. 16.

[201] Ibid., pp. 21-24.

[202] McGee and others, eds., *Sociology: An Introduction,*
p. 22.

[203] Shafeer, *Sociology,* p. 21.

[204] Duberman, Hartjen, *Sociology,* pp. 910.

[205] McGee and others, eds., *Sociology: An Introduction,*
pp. 27-28.

[206] Molana Shah Maghsoud Sadegh Angha, *Dawn*
(Lanham, Maryland: University Press of America,
1989), p. 25.

[207] Idem, *Psalm of God* (Lanham, Maryland: University
Press of America, 1984), p. 4.

[208] Molana Salaheddin Ali Nader Shah Angha, *Secret
Word* (Lanham, Maryland: University Press of
America, 1984), p. 17.

[209] Molana Shah Maghsoud Sadegh Angha, *The Hidden
Angles of Life* (Pomona, CA: Multidisciplinary
Publications, 1975), p. 43.

[210] Ibid., p. 45.

[211] Idem, *Manifestations of Thought* (Lanham, Maryland: University Press of America, 1988), p. 62.

[212] Idem, *The Principles of Faghr and Sufism* (Verdugo City, CA: M.T.O. Shahmaghsoudi Publications, 1987), p. 18.

[213] Ibid. p. 95.

[214] Idem, *Manifestations of Thought*, pp. 17-18.

[215] Ibid., p. 31.

[216] Hazrat Mir Ghotbeddin Mohammed Angha, *From Fetus to Paradise: The Evolutionary States of Man* (Verdugo City, CA: M.T.O. Shahmaghsoudi Publications, 1981), p. 176.

[217] Molana Shah Maghsoud Sadegh Angha, *The Principles of Faghr and Sufism,* p. 111.

[218] Idem, *The Hidden Angles of Life*, p. 60.

[219] Paul Davies, *Other Worlds* (New York: Simon & Schuster, 1980), pp. 3-12.

[220] David Bohm, *Wholeness and the Implicate Order* (London: Routledge, 1995).

[221] Karl Pribram, interview in: *Omni* (Oct. 1982), p.174.

[222] Bohm, *Wholeness and the Implicate Order*, pp. 212-213.

[223] Carl Jung, *Letters, Vol. 2, 1951-1961,* G. Adler, ed. (Princeton, NJ: Princeton University Press, 1975), pp. 194-195.

[224] The conventional Arabic transliteration is Uwais al-Qarani.

[225] Bohm, *Wholeness and the Implicate Order*

[226] William James, *The Principles of Psychology,* 2 Volumes (New York: Holt, Rhineholt, and William, unaltered republication, 1980. New York: Dove, 1950. Volume 1), p. 420.

[227] Karl Jasper, *Spinoza,* from: *The Great Philosophers.*

The Original Thinker series (New York: Harcourt
Brace and Jovanovich, 1974), p. 187.
[228] Nahjol Fessaheh, *Muhammad, the Holy Prophet*,
p. 108.
[229] James Robinson, ed., *The Nag Hammadi Library*,
Institute for Antiquity and Christianity (New York:
Harper & Row, 1977), p. 126.
[230] Molana Shah Maghsoud Sadegh Angha, *Dawn*, p. 29.
[231] Duberman, Hartjen, *Sociology*, pp. 120-121.
[232] Ibid., p. 116.
[233] Ibid., pp. 214-217.
[234] John P. Dworetzky, *Psychology* (New York: West,
1985), p. 238.
[235] Ibid., p. 202.
[236] Molana Shah Maghsoud Sadegh Angha, *Al-Rasa'el*,
(Lanham, Maryland: University Press of America,
1986), p. 79.
[237] Idem, *Dawn*, p. 29.
[238] The Human Body (New York: Reader's Digest Path-
finders), pp. 52-53.
[239] Aldous Huxley, *The Human Situation* (London:
Triad Ganada, 1980), p. 172.
[240] Robert Ornstein quoted from Philip Hilts, *Memory
Ghost: The Strange Tale of Mr. M and the Nature of
Memory* (New York: Simon & Schuster, 1995), p. 222.
[241] Bohm, *Wholeness and the Implicate Order*, pp.
143-147.
[242] Ibid., p. 140.
[243] Karl Pribram, Interview in: *Omni*, p. 172.
[244] Ibid., p. 172.
[245] Ibid., p. 84.
[246] Bohm, *Wholeness and the Implicate Order*,
pp. 212-213.
[247] Molana Shah Maghsoud Sadegh Angha, *The*

Mystery of Humanity: Survival and Tranquility
(Lanham, Maryland: University Press of America,
1996).

248 Idem, *Dawn.*

249 Idem, *Message from the Soul,* reprinted in: idem, *The
Mystery of Humanity: Survival and Tranquility*
(Lanham, Maryland: University Press of America,
1996), pp. 63-64.

250 G.M.A. Grube (trans.), *The Republic of Plato* (India-
napolis: Hackett, 1974), pp. 170-171.

251 Hilts, *Memory Ghost: The Strange Tale of Mr. M and
the Nature of Memory,* p. 22.

252 Ibid.

253 Sir Arthur Eddington, *The Nature of the Physical
World* (New York: MacMillan, 1929), cited in: Ken
Weber, *Quantum Questions: Mystical Writings of
the World's Greatest Physicists* (Boulder, CO:
Shambhala Press, 1984), p. 9.

254 Robinson, ed., *The Nag Hammadi Library,* p. 120.

255 Molana Shah Maghsoud Sadegh Angha, *Al-Rasa'el,*
p. 38.

256 Ibid., pp. 38-39.

257 Ibid., p. 91.

258 Jalal-Ud-Din Rumi, *Mathnawi.*

259 Porras, Silver, *Organization Development*, p. 99.

260 Margaret J. Wheatley, *Leadership and the New
Science* (San Francisco: Berrett - Koehler, 1994), p. 6.

261 Ibid., p. 8.

262 Molana Shah Maghsoud Sadegh Angha, *The Hidden
Angles of Life*, p. 60.

263 Ken Wilbur, *The Holographic Paradigm and Other
Paradoxes* (Boulder, CO: Shambhala Press, 1985),
p. 2.

264 Wheatley, *Leadership and the New Science,*

pp. 121-122.

265 Molana Shah Maghsoud Sadegh Angha, *Al-Rasa'el*, p. 26.

266 Sheikh Izzidin, quoted in the preface to Al-Muqaddisi, *Revelation of the Secrets of the Birds and Flowers* (London: Octagon Press, 1980).

267 Molana Shah Maghsoud Sadegh Angha, *The Principles of Faghr and Sufism*, p. 10.

268 Idem, *Dawn*, p. 27.

269 Idem, *The Principles of Faghr and Sufism*, p. 64.

270 Hazrat Mir Ghotbeddin Mohammad Angha, *From Fetus to Paradise: The Evolutionary States of Man*, Introduction, p. 6.

Index

A

Abbasid Empire 75
ability 20, 32, 41, 57
Abraham 194
Acceptance Theory of
    Authority 23
Adam 194
Amir-al Moemenin Ali
    146, 172, 196,
Angha, Mir Ghotbeddin
    Mohammad 200
Angha, Sadegh 117, 121,
    126, 128, 139, 151, 158,
    162, 163, 165, 173, 186,
    187, 188, 197, 199
Ardebili, Safieddin 173
Arif 169, 173, 175
Arthur, Brian 51
Artificial Intelligence
    (AI) 49
astrophysics 119
attraction 137, 185, 187,
    191, 192
    field of attraction
    138-141, 185, 186,
    190-193, 198

authoritarian 74, 76, 77,
    82, 87, 88, 101, 104
authority 17-21, 25, 29, 30,
    76, 86, 102, 113
awareness 132, 174

B

Babbage, Charles 13
Bagher, Mohammad 198
balance 21, 57, 58, 69,
    72, 81, 83, 92, 109,
    112, 119, 121-125, 129,
    131, 134, 148, 154, 174,
    183-185, 187, 190, 195
    196, 202
Barnard, Chester 23-25, 37,
Bastami, Bayazid 194
behavior 18, 21, 27-31, 42,
    47, 59-61, 63, 65, 71, 72
    104, 107-109, 112, 113,
    116, 120, 132, 152, 153,
    175, 185, 195
Bible 166
biology 23, 37, 119, 171,
    182, 184

L

La-ilaha-il'Allah 196
laws 195
Le Pen 95
leadership 15, 30, 40, 41,
    42, 64, 117, 136, 182,
    184, 198
Levy, A. 63, 175
life span 152
logic 130, 155, 174,
love 64, 131, 133, 137,
147,
    174, 191, 196
    real love 139
    ordinary love 138

M

m-commerce 49
M.T.O. Shahmaghsoudi
    School of Sufism
    165, 197
magnetic field 140, 168,
186,
    187, 192
magnetism 141, 165
Malone, Michael S. 58
management 129

management, principles
    of 19

Mao Tse-tung 86
Marx, Karl 111-113, 115
Marxism-Leninism 82, 83,
    87
Maslow, Abraham 27, 28, 30
materialism 149, 183
mathematics 33
matter 186, 190,
Mayo, George Elton 26, 27,
    31, 43
McGregor, Douglas 29-31,
McNelly, Theodore 100
Mead, George Herbert 115
medicine 119, 166, 168
meditation 63, 168, 174,
    175, 193
memory 151, 156-158,
    160, 170
Merrill, Harwood F. 24
Merry, V. 63, 175
Metcalfe, Henry 13
military 18, 73, 74, 76,
    77-79, 84, 93, 96
mind 145, 149, 155, 157,
    172, 175, 192, 193
mission 47, 59, 61, 62
Modern Conflict Theory 115

S

saints 172, 194
Saudi Arabia 79
Scandinavia 96, 98
science 9
scientific management 13,
    178
scientific method 9, 22
secularism 103
security 66
self 28, 58, 144, 145,
    174, 199
    self-discipline 174, 201
    self-discovery 145, 163,
        174
    self-knowledge 136,
        145, 146, 169, 178, 185,
        192, 197, 201
    selfishness 129
sensory science 159, 161
shared vision 64, 137,
    177, 185
Silver, Robert C. 60
skills 15, 130, 151, 166
social
    social context 22, 24, 25,
        114, 120, 137, 178
    social factors 59, 61,
        108, 132, 152

social groups 125
social interaction
    43, 53, 59
social man 24, 58, 178
social structure 60, 111
social system 24, 39,
    112, 114
socialism 82, 87, 103
socialization 152
society 73, 126, 132, 135,
    177, 182, 184, 185, 201,
    202
sociology 60, 107, 110,
    114, 152, 153
soul 150, 174, 192
source of life 70, 132, 135,
    140, 145, 150, 165, 167,
    187, 190, 199
Soviet Union 82, 83, 99
space 184, 185, 187
space and time 113,
    119, 123
specialization 20, 73, 92
Spinoza 150
spiritual 39, 131, 138,
    144-146, 149, 163, 173,
    189, 197, 201
    spiritual evolution 164
    spiritual training 169
stability 119, 121, 131, 141,

V

values 17, 43, 54, 65, 94,
    103, 107, 110, 120, 123
    inherent value 117, 120,
    130, 132, 153, 201
vision 60, 140, 171, 191
Vroom, Victor 28

W

wavelength 134, 157
Weber, Max 17, 30, 112
welfare 26, 30, 89, 98, 178
well-being 39, 124, 131,
    164, 184
willingness 15, 46, 57
wisdom 29, 66, 67, 122,
    123, 131, 155, 163,
    198, 201
work setting 61

Z

Zoroaster 194

Also by the same author:

Expansion &
Contraction
Within Being

Professor Nader Angha
485 pages
ISBN 0-910735-61-1
£ 24.99

Do you ever wonder why the universe is expanding and
what the relationship of that expansion is to living
beings? Have you ever wondered if humanity will ever
find a cure for debilitating diseases such as cancer and
AIDS? Ever wondered what the relationship of the
conscious and unconscious mind is to the brain?

This book is a showcase of Professor Angha's mastery
of the sciences, particularly Biology and Physics. It is
a metriculous presentation of the unity of the being and
presents a fresh view of the essence within.

All MTO Publications' titles can be ordered from your
local bookshop.